INTEGRATED POLLUTION MANAGEMENT

Integrated Pollution Management

Improving Environmental Performance

FRANK FEATES

Professor of Environmental Technology
University of Manchester Institute
of Science and Technology

ROD BARRATT

Environmental Engineering Group
Faculty of Technology
The Open University

McGRAW-HILL BOOK COMPANY

London · New York · St Louis · San Francisco · Auckland
Bogotá · Caracas · Lisbon · Madrid · Mexico · Montreal
New Delhi · Panama · Paris · San Juan · São Paulo
Singapore · Sydney · Tokyo · Toronto

Published by
McGraw-Hill Book Company Europe
Shoppenhangers Road, Maidenhead, Berkshire SL6 2QL, England
Telephone 01628 23432
Facsimile 01628 770224

British Library Cataloguing in Publication Data

Feates, Frank
  Integrated Pollution Management:
  Improving Environmental Performance
  I. Title   II. Barratt, Rod
  628.5

  ISBN 0-07-707867-5

Library of Congress Cataloging-in-Publication Data

Feates, Frank S.
  Integrated pollution management: improving environmental
performance / Frank Feates, Rod Barratt.
    p. cm.
  Includes index.
  ISBN 0-07-707867-5
  1. Industrial management—Environmental aspects. I. Barratt,
Rod. II. Title.
  HD30.255.F43   1994
  658.4′08—dc20
                                                            94-44157
                                                            CIP

1 2 3 4 5 BL 9 8 7 6 5

Typeset by Paston Press Ltd, Loddon, Norfolk
Printed and Bound in Great Britain by Biddles Ltd, Guildford, Surrey

Printed on permanent paper in compliance with the ISO Standard 9706

Contents

Preface

This book has been written for managers who wish to learn more about the environmental performance of their activities and plant, and how to make improvements. It also provides detailed information on how they can meet the growing social, regulatory and market pressures to which they are subject, and gain competitive advantage.

However, environmental performance is not only of concern to industrial and other business managers. It also is of wider interest to students and members of the general public who are increasingly questioning the 'Green' image of the organizations with which they deal and of the products they buy. Environmentally aware customers, whether individual or corporate, present an increasing challenge to organizations that cannot be ignored. This book will assist them all in learning a little more of what environmental performance is, and how it can be measured, assessed and improved. We recognize that many of our readers will not have a degree in Environmental Science, and so we have endeavoured to present the text as free as is practicable of technical jargon and mathematics. However, there are some acronyms which have entered the language of environmental protection, and where we introduce them we offer full explanations. A brief glossary is also provided at the end of the book.

Our approach has been to move systematically through from a very superficial environmental audit to regulatory matters and finally to means of monitoring and improving performance. We have also chosen a structure with a number of self-contained chapters, any of which can be read independently, as can the Case Studies illustrating points and approaches described in the main text. This structure means a little repetition for which we offer no apology. There are concepts which gain strength from being repeated, often in a slightly different way to illustrate a particular point. We consider that this adds to reader interest as well as reinforcing key arguments and demonstrating positive benefits.

There are as many ways of dealing with an environmental issue as there are critics of it. Inevitably there is no unique solution, and this we have tried to stress. However, we have followed an approach based on integrated pollution management which, we believe, has much to commend it, and appears to be the way forward in most developed countries.

We have also sought to keep this book relatively short as well as readable. It would not be difficult to produce a 10-volume treatise on pollution management, and some authors have done so. However, such tomes can only serve as reference manuals, and have the major disadvantage that with changes in legislative practices and improvements in pollution abatement technology they rapidly become out of date. We have tried to concentrate in this book on principles rather than list state of the art techniques and trust that it will stand the test of time. As the approaches we describe are becoming established at international level we also consider that this book has much to offer readers outside the UK, although inevitably much of the background arises from our UK experiences.

For the reader who wants more detail, or specific information, a selected number of references have been included which we have found to be particularly useful, and an Appendix with the names of key organizations which can supply more detailed or specific information.

Acknowledgements

The authors thank Alan Windsor, previously head of the HMIP North Region, for assistance in formulating the structure of this book and helpful advice at the conceptual stage.

They are also indebted to the following individuals and organizations for help in preparing the text, and for permission to use proprietary information: ABB ASEA Brown Boveri, Aspinwall and Co, Ltd, BP plc, British Nuclear Fuels, Chemical Industries Association, S. Grunden (Waste), HMIP, ICI plc, March Consulting Group, The Open University, M. Sellars (ICI Acrylics), Siemens Plessey Controls.

We also appreciate the forbearance shown by our families during the time taken in writing this book.

1

Concepts: The New Approach

'I never measure my discharges so I am not aware that I cause any pollution.'

'I only take remedial action to reduce discharges in response to formal complaints by my regulators.'

'Wastes are no real concern of our company—someone comes when necessary and takes away whatever we give him.'

'Environmental issues aren't relevant to our business—we should stick to what we know.'

How many times have you heard comments such as these? We suspect all too often in the past. Managers who made such comments cared little about the problems they could be building up for their successors, or the long-term financial consequences for the owners or shareholders of the organization, quite apart from admitting that they had no full understanding of the process or plant for which they were formally responsible. The main concerns were 'are we legal?' and 'what's in it for us?'

This book casts managers in a different mould: the responsible environmentalists or, maybe, those who recognize that they have for too long followed the no-see no-care philosophy outlined in our opening. They will wish to reshape the company's business approach to the environment and to pollution. They recognize that not only will the company then be seen as environmentally aware but also that real financial savings may well result, rather than unnecessary costs resulting from unco-ordinated responses to the ever-increasing pressures of regulators world-wide, the market-place and social atttitudes. We can draw a parallel with the total quality management. Organizations are increasingly moving towards formal accreditation of their management systems, for instance from standards like BS5750 and ISO9000 which we describe in Chapter 3. Similar pressures are likely to drive integration of environmental management into the corporate culture. Even non-manufacturing organizations such as retailing and the financial sector are taking environmental issues seriously, with resulting pressures being applied more widely through the supply chain.

What we aim to achieve is an appreciation of all the factors the modern manager should be able to take into account in designing, commissioning, operating and eventually closing a plant which has some potential to create pollution. The plant does not have to be obviously polluting. For example, the local dry cleaning shop employing chlorinated solvents and a timber-yard using wood preservatives need the same type of consideration as a major chemical plant, but not, of course, in the same depth or to the same degree. Similar arguments apply to any product or service, which must increasingly be designed with regard to the environmental implications over the whole life cycle of its use. This view must also take in ancillary aspects such as packaging. It will be for the individual manager to decide which factors are relevant to the company's activities and then develop an analysis to accommodate them. We are convinced that the logical approach which we are proposing will give greater confidence in justifying the attitude adopted to senior management, to the regulators and to customers. The bonus coming from optimization of pollution control will manifest itself in reduced additional costs—and often in reduced actual costs—as well as protecting the work-force, the local and general public, and the environment generally from any undesirable consequences of management decisions. Perhaps one of the most powerful driving forces to many will be the product differentiation in a commercial market-place that is becoming increasingly environmentally aware. Environmental concerns are not a passing phase, and organizations that have the vision to identify the opportunities and take appropriate action will be assured of a profitable and sustainable future.

In this chapter we are going to concentrate on setting out the concepts of our approach, and demonstrate the types of question and commitment the concerned managers should be asking themselves, their work-force, and their boards of directors. We will show how the answers can be obtained in the subsequent chapters, with real examples based on the experience of others and ourselves.

Integrated Pollution Management

The key to Integrated Pollution Management, which we will abbreviate to IPM, is the recognition that the pollution potential of any plant is regarded in exactly the same way as the effective manager has traditionally treated costs and profitability. Just as an effective financial manager looks for ways to reduce costs and increase profitability in all aspects of business activity, so the effective environmental manager looks at pollution potential. It is important to recognize potential pollution, since it is a manager's duty always to consider 'what if?' and to be satisfied that any consequences can be dealt with.

- What if we decide to increase through-put? Do we have the capacity to deal with the additional waste products?
- What if the pollution control equipment fails? Do we have to shut the plant down to meet our discharge consents?
- What if we ignore IPM? Will our customers seek other suppliers, will we be able to secure funding from the banks, and will we be able to insure our liabilities?
- What if we change our raw materials? Do we have new and expensive pollution problems to deal with?
- What if we reduce a discharge to the local river, but increase our gaseous emissions and our solid waste? How do the environmental consequences compare?

There is a diversity of ways in which these factors can be taken into account. The way we suggest is based very much on the pioneering work done in the United Kingdom during the 1980s in developing the concepts of Integrated Pollution Control (IPC) which now forms the backbone to modern pollution management in the British Isles. One of us was closely associated with the formulation and initial implementation of IPC and we make no apology for referring primarily to our experiences with it. It is widely regarded as a model for other countries, and is being developed still further for pan-European adoption as Integrated Pollution Prevention and Control (IPPC). Our colleagues in the Americas, Asia and Australia have all shown great interest and the approach really does have global application, if only to demonstrate a logical and rigorous approach to the duty of industry to help protect our environment.

However this book is not an account of IPC as practised in the UK. It is a development from IPC which we consider brings together a wider range of environmental factors than have been tackled before. In practice, it is unlikely that any regulatory framework could encompass the range of factors we are proposing, but that does not stop the individual manager from considering them all in developing a strategy for the particular situation faced by the company in question. Without a doubt there will be many items which need not be pursued, but at least there will be a rationale for justifying decisions to anybody who asks for them.

Inputs and Outputs

So, what are we to do and where do we begin? First and foremost we must analyse the environmental consequences of our organization's activities from beginning to end. This does not necessarily mean undertaking a full life cycle analysis (LCA) of activities, but certainly it is not enough simply to start where the raw materials enter the first production stage and end when the finished product leaves the last stage. For instance, we also need to know something of the origins of our raw materials. B&Q, a large UK do-it-yourself retail chain, now requires all its suppliers to provide evidence that their products have been produced in an environmentally sensitive way. More and more companies are requiring similar statements from suppliers, and one case in point concerns certification that no ozone depleting chemicals (such as chlorofluorocarbons or CFCs) have been used at any point in the life cycle of a product. The example in Chapter 8, Section 3, illustrates this pressure on organizations. Similarly, more than 30 banks from around the world have signed a statement including the expectation that:

'. . . as part of our normal business practices, that our customers comply with all applicable local, national and international environmental regulations. Beyond compliance, we regard sound environmental practices as one of the key factors demonstrating effective corporate management.'

UN Statement by Banks on Environment and Sustainable Development, 1992

Coming now into our activity or plant, we need to know how the raw materials are stored on site, and if we have such large quantities that they could pose an unnecessarily large hazard in the case of a fire or other accident. Are bulk supplies protected from weathering and possible leaching of polluting liquors?

After our industrial activity or other involvement is finished what will be the end use of our product or service? Could it cause global pollution like CFCs? Could it be manufactured without using environmentally deleterious chemicals, such as certain chlorinated organic compounds or 'heavy metals' (development of unleaded fuels and mercury-free batteries for instance). Can the product be dismantled easily so that components can be recycled? This is now a stated aim of several major vehicle manufacturers. Are there particular problems in disposing of the product at the end of its useful life? The case with CFC-charged refrigeration plant is one example, while packaging materials are a growing concern. Case studies dealing with both topics are included in Chapter 8. Are packaging materials minimized and recycled when practicable, as new German legislation requires? Are waste disposal routes available? This is a long-term problem that the international nuclear power industry has been forced to come to terms with!

Concerns over life cycle concepts and design for the environment are increasingly deserving attention in all departments of organizations, from research and development, through manufacturing to marketing and even in support services (Figure 1.1). Environmental concerns are no longer the exclusive responsibility of technical personnel in manufacturing industry.

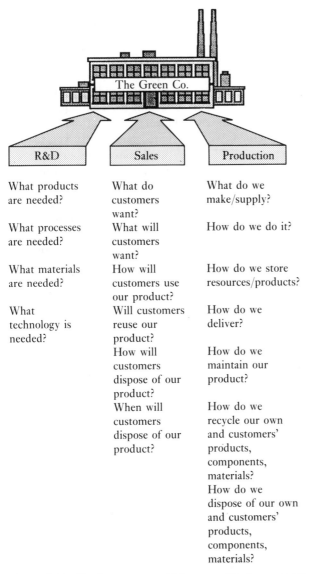

R&D	Sales	Production
What products are needed?	What do customers want?	What do we make/supply?
What processes are needed?	What will customers want?	How do we do it?
What materials are needed?	How will customers use our product?	How do we store resources/products?
What technology is needed?	Will customers reuse our product?	How do we deliver?
	How will customers dispose of our product?	How do we maintain our product?
	When will customers dispose of our product?	How do we recycle our own and customers' products, components, materials?
		How do we dispose of our own and customers' products, components, materials?

Figure 1.1   The Organization with Integrated Environmental Management

Know Your Plant

The points illustrated above are just some of the peripheral factors you need to show you have considered. We will be exploring these in more detail later in the book, but remember that not all, indeed, probably not many will be of direct relevance to your activity. But what of the process which you manage? That is clearly your prime concern. What factors do you need to take into account?

One approach could be to employ a consultant to carry out a so-called 'Environmental Audit'. The consultant could spend a day or two looking at your plant, talk to some of the managers or operators and produce a report telling you how to spend large capital sums to gain minimal improvements. You would know little more about the environmental effects of your plant than you knew before the work started. We strongly recommend that you take the lead in assessing your own plant. You may need consultants to guide you through new concepts, or to develop models and make complex calculations, but always keep in the driving seat. Let the consultant help you, by all means, but you do need to learn everything you can about the environmental aspects of your operations. A contractor's Environmental Report is not adequate.

Let us first assume that you are starting to build your plant on a green-field site. First and foremost you have to establish the local environmental situation.

- How deep is the groundwater? Where does it flow and what aquifers or watercourses does it feed? A recent landmark in legal case history illustrates the potential consequences of not being aware of these potential problems, and we summarize some of its key points in Chapter 8, Section 1.
- What is the prevailing wind direction and where is there human habitation or habitats of animals or rare plant species? Are there hills to influence dispersion of atmospheric discharges?
- Can solid wastes be safely buried on the site or must they be shipped away? What is the transport infrastructure?

Many other features of the site will also require investigation: some to satisfy planning requirements but many others of a strictly environmental nature. We will be considering these in depth later in the book.

When the plant is to be built you will need to ensure that adequate space has been assigned for the pollution abatement systems which the process demands. This book will help you to see what is available and how it may work in your situation. This, in turn, should assist you in discussions with your regulators who will expect you to have surveyed a wide range of pollution options and selected the 'Best Available Techniques' (BAT) in your Integrated Pollution Management approach. You will also have considered trade-offs between alternatives which lead to discharges to different media: air, water, landfill are examples. You will have to decide how to compare the environmental consequences of the options, perhaps by finding the pathways by which pollutants reach humans and the environment, and then assessing the harm that will result from each of the options. Our discussion in Chapter 4 of means to select the Best Practicable Environmental Option (BPEO) will help you with the methodology for undertaking this task, which can easily appear daunting to those unfamiliar with it.

We must not neglect the operation of the industrial process itself. Are staff adequately trained in the environmental aspects of their work? Have you shown them that the statements in the first sentences of this chapter are not consistent with your environmental policy? Indeed, do you have an agreed environmental policy and have you written a company Environmental Statement and explained it to all your work-force? Do you also have a management structure to implement the policy and directed at achieving the objectives? Examples of how (and how not) to deal with these matters are given in Chapters 3 and 8.

Have steps been taken to minimize waste? For instance, Rolls-Royce (1972) Ltd managed to reduce a high value metal waste by a factor of 10 by moving from casting to powder sintering, with consequential reductions in power requirements and raw material purchases. Can cleaner technology be employed? The UK Department of Trade and Industry (DTI) has instituted prizes for companies which have been most successful in introducing cleaner technology. The details of the awards make instructive reading, demonstrating the very short payback times of many of the most successful innovations.[1]

Is there adequate monitoring for process control from an environmental standpoint, and are all discharges being measured adequately? Can the discharge monitoring results be used directly for process control in a feedback arrangement as is now done with many incinerators and boiler plant? Are better monitoring instruments available at acceptable cost to increase the speed and accuracy of measurement? Chapter 5 illustrates what can be done to measure your environmental performance.

The Environmental Impact

Having collected the extensive range of information about your raw materials, plant and product you are now faced with the task of assessing the true environmental impact and satisfying yourself that it has been minimized in a cost-effective manner. How will we measure environmental impact? There are several ways, each of which has its own advantages and disadvantages.

The easiest way is to rely on our senses. Can we see pollution, can we smell it or are there other visible signs such as dead fish floating in the local river? These are obvious examples and represent the traditional method of assessment, but we are now becoming more sophisticated and looking for the less obvious signs of pollution. Often these cannot be measured directly, and can only be obtained by extrapolation from other scenarios, by mathematical modelling or by epidemiological studies. Measurement is the key to all such approaches and the basic data collected from monitoring give us our inputs.

Perhaps it is easiest to consider a risk ranking and successively satisfy ourselves that the risks at each level are acceptably low. We suggest the following:

- Health and safety of workers
- Health and amenity of the local 'most exposed' population
- Health of more distant populations at national and international levels
- Preservation of rare and endangered species, animal and plant
- Visual, aural or nasal intrusion (ugly stacks, noisy plant, nasty smells)
- Other factors, including transport effects, loss of amenity, etc.

Remember that the work-force are generally the healthy members of the community, while those not at work include the old, the sick and the very young, all of whom may be more susceptible to harm from environmental problems. Clearly it is important to assess immediate effects first, but we must also take into account delayed effects, which could stretch over many generations. For instance, leachate from some landfill sites closed many years ago are only now reaching watercourses and causing pollution. Similarly, consider the harm caused by accidental spillage entering an aquifer (see the example in Chapter 8, Section 1). How do we compare this type of risk with that resulting from immediate discharges into a stream? How do we balance risks to humans with risks to other animals or, indeed, plants? Are there synergistic effects, such that two pollutants mixed together cause more harm than the sum of the two separately? There remains much to be done in setting out a methodology for making these choices, but a critical group approach along these lines has been very successful in the nuclear industry and is described in Chapter 4.

Another factor we have to consider is the comparison between a continuing low pollution potential and a scenario where the general polluting level is even lower, but occasional excursions lead to transients with more significant consequences. For example, how do we balance a stack with a continuous slight plume against one with no plume under normal circumstances, but which for very short periods emits dense black smoke as the plant starts up? Whereas the integrated pollution levels may be the same in both cases, generally regulators and the public prefer the former situation to the latter.

The full analysis of the risks set out above should allow the manager to reach a view on the true pollution potential of the activity or plant. If this is done for several options at the design and reconstruction phases in the history of the plant then the manager can also justify selection of a BPEO, the key feature of the integrated approach.

In Search of Total Quality

Having selected our BAT and our BPEO we have the task of satisfying ourselves that the standards are maintained and the records are adequate. The good manager therefore has to institute auditable systems for quality control and quality checking. Here professional institutions and the national standards institutes have a role to play, and they are addressed in Chapter 3. In the UK the major professional and trade associations have given guidance to their members on quality standards and how they are to be applied. Environmental quality is part of total quality management, and acceptance of the former is bound to grow in a similar manner to the widespread acceptance of quality. Preventing pollution by design has a parallel in the quality concept of preventing defects by design. No longer is the view held that higher quality in products and processes automatically increases costs. Products, processes and activities designed with pollution prevention and waste minimization in mind will probably cost less overall than the traditional end-of-pipe clean-up approach. It has been said that 'environmentalism, like the quality movement, challenges companies to do what's good for them'.[2] These quality concepts will be discussed in more detail in Chapter 3.

Practical Points for Action

- Consider formal accreditation of management systems.
- Develop an integrated approach to pollution abatement and environmental control.
- Ask key questions about the running of your plant—waste avoidance, recycling, energy generation—and disposal.
- Know your inputs and outputs. Is the difference avoidable waste?
- What will happen to the plant at the end of its design life: are there environmental implications to upgrading or decommissioning?
- Develop knowledge about the pollutants generated by your process, and how they may harm humans and the environment.

References

1   *Cutting your Losses* and *Cutting your Losses 2*. Department of Trade & Industry Enterprise Initiative, Bridge Place, 88/89 Eccleston Square, London SW11V 1PT.
2   A. Kleiner, 'What does it mean to be green', *Harvard Business Review*, July–August 1991, 38.

2

Constraints

What are the significant issues for your organization?

Your list may differ from ours in its order, but it is likely to include:

- Compliance now
- Compliance in the future
- Civil litigation
- Capital and revenue expenditure
- Public and customer concerns
- Poor management of resources, raw materials or waste
- Strategic development
- Validity of insurance
- Releases to the environment

Management Attitudes Towards Environmental Issues

Compliance is likely to be at the head of the list reflecting the immediate concerns of people in most organizations as: 'Are we legal?', followed by: 'How much does it cost?', 'What are the benefits?'

Environmental issues have assumed a high profile at various times throughout history, but while the concerns have changed over the years, so too have the perspectives. In an 1833 essay, 'The Tragedy of the Commons', William Forster Lloyd described the relentless decline of the common good caused by individual farmers each seeking personal gain from using the town commons for grazing. As every farmer thought likewise, there was overuse and eventual erosion of the commons.

In the past, environmental protection pressures have all too often been considered as constraints; unnecessary pressures drawing attention away from the main business purpose, and squeezing limited resources (Figure 2.1). Managers in organizations dismissed their own environmental lapses as insignificant in the overall picture and limited themselves to correcting negative

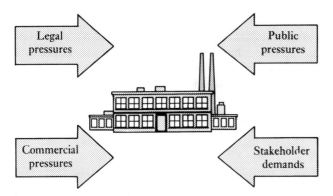

Figure 2.1   External pressures operating to improve the environmental performance of organizations

aspects as each problem arose; they were particularly concerned about the cost of corrective action. Often the costs of preventing pollution were considered excessive and the benefits too distant.

The evolution of public and commercial awareness and the underpinning of legal and social pressures now present the environment as an opportunity for business activity. In commercial terms the world environmental market has been estimated as worth more than the global aerospace industry,[1] yet many firms do not appear to be aware of the nature of the opportunities and how to exploit them. The key is to move from a situation in which negative aspects of each problem are addressed with an emphasis on costs to an active environmental management phase with the environment being recognized as an area of opportunity. Pollution prevention is recognized as better than combating it. The next evolutionary phase integrates the behaviour of an enterprise with the environment, and preventing environmental problems is recognized as the result of integrating environmental considerations into normal good management practice.

A recent picture of management attitudes to environmental issues comes from a survey carried out in eight European countries in 1990.[2] The overall conclusion was that the UK appeared to be behind its European partners in developing proactive positions on environmental issues, with only 50 per cent of UK companies having board level involvement, and only one-third having an environmental policy. Indeed, some UK companies claimed that their activities had no effect on the environment, whereas all other EU companies surveyed recognized some environmental impact. Future legislation was seen generally as likely to have considerable impact on all aspects of business, with German and Dutch companies believing that their own national legislation would continue to be more demanding than that of the EU. Perhaps reflecting this, the most strategic approach to environmental issues was evident in the

Netherlands, while the impact of the environmentally aware consumer was greatest in Germany. Pressure from shareholders, insurers and banks was virtually non-existent in the UK. This snapshot of business attitudes presents only part of an evolving picture, and evolution is inevitable as a result of the constraints acting on organizations. Indeed, a later survey of British management attitudes revealed that 94 per cent of respondents expected environmental pressures to increase, and 53 per cent would consider introducing an environmental management system.[3]

Multinational companies set examples

Environmental management has the normal management problems of planning, dealing with resources and managing people who are resistant to change and may be confused about their roles in relation to what they perceive to be global problems. In addition there are technical issues and the inevitable jargon. These difficulties make environmental issues appear daunting.

Evidence of a changing culture is apparent in statements by large company leaders:

'Doing business efficiently and effectively in a mere technocratic sense is no longer sufficient to preserve the acceptability of business by society.'

Chairman of Ciba-Geigy, quoted in *Financial Times* 21 September 1989

The Chairman of Ciba-Geigy added that 'environmental considerations had to become an integral part of the managerial decision-making process in many companies. Industry might have to make "social and financial sacrifices" if it was to deal adequately with environmental issues. Nor should companies wait for government authorities to draw up regulations.'

Another view is:

'Good environmental performance is not an option. It is essential if ICI is to continue as a leading international chemical company into the next century.'

Sir Denys Henderson, Chairman ICI, *ICI Policy Document on the Environment*, July 1991

To these we can add:

Making a profit is a necessity, but it should not be allowed to mean sidestepping our environmental responsibilities. A positive approach to environmental questions is also a competitive advantage. Environmental, occupational and produce safety issues call for continuous attention and vigilance in all of Neste's business areas. For us to be efficient and alert to these issues, individuals at all levels should be aware of their responsibility in this area.

The Neste way of working, Neste Corporation, Finland

The quotations cited here are merely a few of those recognizing the opportunities of environmental management. The first identifies anticipating regulatory constraints, but as the last quotation suggests, recognition of environmental issues by the leaders must be followed through by action involving everyone. Unfortunately, environmental issues are often presented as global problems and while this may be true, it tends to suggest that individual actions are likely to be insignificant. Ways of addressing these communication issues will be covered in Chapters 3 and 7. Here we will start with the global picture in which multinational organizations operate.

A Global Perspective

The environment does not respect national boundaries drawn on maps, and activities that harm the environment of one country may also cause harm elsewhere. This wide dimension presents challenges to politicians to reconcile the priorities and goals of different communities and cultures.

Since the Industrial Revolution in the UK, technological change and economic growth have generated controversy, and this has grown with the recognition of the environmental degradation that has followed the advance of the industrial economy. One line of argument proposes that this advance will also offer a solution to pollution. From the other end of the spectrum of views would come the argument that the only solution involves a radical change in the capitalist system that depends on competition, growth and resource consumption. Political changes in recent years suggest that neither extreme has the winning position, since capitalism and communism have both imposed severe demands on the natural environment.

Our increasingly global systems are transforming the world into groups, and this is no less apparent than in economic systems. Competitive advantage, a fundamental building block of capitalism, has been absorbed into the vocabulary of the organizations which see the environment not as a threat but as a business opportunity. Environmental problems are predominantly associated with technical issues, and for every technical problem there is perceived to be a technical solution. Of course, there are trade-offs in terms of costs in production and costs to customers which must be balanced against environmental benefits. However, this view of technical solutions alone offering a panacea and that everything is possible at a price is naive.

Since the 1950s there has been a growing groundswell of environmental concern which led to the first UN International Conference on the Environment in 1972 in Stockholm. Some arguments of the time proposed that technological developments in the form of nuclear power offered the prospect of no energy shortages in the future. At the other extreme, the whole of nature is placed above the human race in importance, and such a utopian ethos demands no growth as the solution to environmental problems. Growth and development are, of course, value-laden terms and require value-judgements by people representing the whole spectrum of opinions. We could argue that industrial economies have proved themselves to be remarkably adaptable and resilient as a form of economic development, and these very qualities offer the capacity for technology to rise to the environmental challenges. Against this view is the perception that many of the world's environmental problems are growing, and that technological solutions have to be proven. Unfortunately, growth and development are often used together and tend to be regarded as synonymous, but whereas growth implies a quantitative expansion of the economic system, development incorporates qualitative ideas of improvement. Development also includes cultural and social dimensions as well as the economic one. We have, then, a consideration of environmental issues depending on scientific and technical evidence but also involving social perceptions, with values being central to any debate.

Over the past two decades, there has been an 'environmental awakening' of politicians which some have attributed to changing values in societies of the developed world. Doubts about the quality of life and the price that industrial economies demanded of the environment in its widest sense were fuelled by growing scientific evidence of environmental problems. Recognition since 1984 of the significant loss of stratospheric ozone over Antarctica with the onset of the austral spring was soon linked irrefutably to the presence of chlorine atoms derived from chlorofluorocarbons (CFCs). These chemicals were hailed as a technological success when they were developed, owing to their stability and non-toxic effects, and so found widespread use in spray cans and refrigeration. Their environmental significance took a long time to be recognized, but once it was, the political response soon followed. The Montreal Protocol was signed in 1987, and was the first international agreement to restrict the release of CFCs into the atmosphere. But despite the scientific evidence, ratification and agreement brought problems in terms of the pressures on developing countries which manufactured the substances, and on industries using them. Our third case study in Chapter 8 shows how a major company has developed a strategy for phasing out their use.

More difficult to resolve have been other issues known familiarly as acid deposition and global warming. These and other problems such as toxic wastes, radioactive waste and pollution of the seas, present conflicts between scientific evidence and political action. To both politicians and industrialists challenging questions involve asking when is there sufficient evidence to do something and what to do? The scientific uncertainties provide loopholes for avoiding issues and taking no action. The resulting policies may have far-reaching social and economic consequences.

Among the other significant events of the 1980s must be counted the UN Commission on Environment and Development (UNCED), also known after its chairperson Mrs Gro Brundtland, the Prime Minister of Norway. The

Brundtland Commission's report entitled *Our Common Future*,[4] published in 1987, resulted from a continuing discussion of environmental issues among many developing and developed countries and including many non-governmental organizations and groups. The mandate for the Commission was to focus on the environment while not ignoring population pressures, differences between rich and poor countries, the need for technology transfer, and the way they are all linked together. This combination of environment and development linked with economy, ecology and poverty was addressed through the holistic concept of sustainable development. This concept has been defined as 'development that meets the needs of the present without compromising the ability of future generations to meet their own needs'. The thrust of UNCED is that a concensus needs to be developed between environmental pressure groups, scientists, politicians and industrialists with the belief that sustainable development offers a key to dealing with the threats to the global environment. Sustainable development goes beyond the traditional conception of environmental protection, and presents an agenda which challenges everyone of us to respond, whether in politics, in business or as individuals in our daily life.

Twenty years after the Stockholm conference in 1972, the UN Conference on Environment and Development, variously known as the Earth Summit or the Rio Summit, took place. Promoted as the largest international gathering ever mounted to debate the global environmental issues, one outcome is known as Agenda 21. This is a global agenda or action plan for the next century. It sets out the international framework for global partnership and for agreements that affect the environment, development and the resources of the planet. Sustainable development is the concept behind the conference declaration, and its vagueness no doubt underpins its popularity among governments and organizations of all persuasions. Agenda 21 sets out to guide governments, businesses and other organizations in their long-term planning. One UK survey[5] of reactions to the summit and its outcomes suggested a generally positive response although little expectation of immediate action. There was general belief that Government should lead by example through actions such as legislating for an environmental market, setting sustainable development goals and providing appropriate finance. Businesses should combine commercial and environmental objectives as well as helping technology transfer to less developed countries, while environmental bodies should collaborate, agree priorities and provide pressure for delivery of commitments. While addressing global issues, Agenda 21 also makes it clear that local action is the key to success.

Following the 1992 conference, many international governments signed a commitment to produce targets on sustainable development to form a Sustainable Development Plan. The UK Plan published in 1994 focuses people's attention 20 years ahead, and poses questions on the status and plausibility of scenarios for that time. In 1997 the Commission on Sustainable Development will review progress of governments' plans as revealed by annual environmental reviews. Increasingly, similar long-term horizons and assessment strategies must be taken by organizations which hitherto have taken shorter perspectives. Only by doing so will the uncertainties of the future be transformed from threats to opportunities.

A wide discussion of sustainable development is outside the scope of this book; rather, the purpose of this outline is to relate the concept as one of the developing constraints on organizations to integrate environmental considerations in their activities. However, it is perhaps worth examining what the Brundtland Report says about the use of energy and materials by industry.

> Industrial growth is widely seen as inevitably accompanied by corresponding increases in energy and raw material consumption. In the past two decades, however, this pattern appears to have changed. As growth has continued in the developed market economies, the demand for many basic materials, including energy and water, has levelled off; in some cases, it has actually declined in absolute terms. The productivity and efficiency of resource use are constantly improving, and industrial production is steadily switching away from heavily material-intensive products and processes. . . . Yet even the most industrially advanced economies still depend on a continued supply of basic manufactured goods. Whether made domestically or imported, their production will continue to require large amounts of raw materials and energy, even if developing countries progress rapidly in the adoption of resource-efficient technologies.

The key elements of energy sustainability that have to be reconciled include accommodating sufficient growth of energy supplies to meet human needs, minimizing waste by improving efficiency, and protecting public health and the biosphere. Integrating environmental management into the corporate culture is clearly a component part of sustainable development.

The sustainable development concept

An overriding merit of the sustainable development concept is that it requires consumers, politicians and the business sector to consider the implications of their decisions many generations beyond the traditional time horizons. We are talking here of far beyond the 'two year payback' which guides many business decisions, and consequently financial managers may need to be persuaded about the long-term benefits of good environmental management so that they do not impede the progress of integrated environmental management within the organization. Table 2.1 compares some features of sustainable development against the traditional approach in terms of the way an international petroleum company approaches the challenges.

The financial benefits are clear from this table, and will be amplified through market advantage and market differentiation by customers. Enlightened managerial attitudes accept the long-term benefits to be gained by adopting

Table 2.1 Aspects of environmental policies. (Adapted from *Economic Growth & the Environment,* Shell International Petroleum Co, 1990)

Unsustainable development	Sustainable development
Policy approach	
'Short-termist'	Forward looking
Uncertainties are divisive and paralyse policy-making	Uncertainties provide fertile ground for research and thought
Research is minimal	Significant research takes place into: the environment technological possibilities policies Precautionary policies are initiated
End product	
Problems become crises	Problems are anticipated
Policies are ill-considered and internally contradictory	Well-considered policies are in place
Extremism overwhelms professional views	Institutions and businesses are geared up
Problems recur	New investment opportunities arise
Profits and growth	
Higher in the short term but lower in the long term	Higher in the longer term
Environment	
Increased costs of clean-up, restoration and maintenance	Generally improved, maintenance costs minimized

long-term environmentally friendly goals in place of short-term profits, although this transformation is difficult in times of financial stress.

Global and local action

Despite long-term awareness of many environmental issues and problems, their formal acknowledgement in the agenda of international and local organizations has often been relatively recent. Before 1 July 1987, the Commission of the European Economic Community had no specific powers in the environmental arena. The Treaty of Rome did not address issues of the environment, environmental protection, pollution and resource depletion, simply because they did not feature on the political agenda in the 1950s. Nevertheless, the European Community made substantial progress in developing legislation to protect the environment even without a specific legal base. Around one hundred different pieces of legislation were enacted covering air, sea, rivers and land, and were based on the need for harmonizing legislation in preparation for the establishment of the single market—to develop a 'level playing field' for business opportunity. The enactment of the Single European Act in the late 1980s provided an explicit base for environment policy, but also introduced a number of important principles including:

> Action by the Community relating to the environment should be based on the principles that preventive action should be taken, that environmental damage should as a priority be rectified at source and that the polluter should pay. Environmental protection requirements shall be a component of the Community's other policies.
>
> Article 130r (2)

Once again the principle of pollution prevention is highlighted, as is integration of environmental issues with other policies, but so too is an implication of costs. The latest Environmental Action Plan from the EU will have significant impact on attitudes and actions on environmental issues. Just as early organizational responses to the environment were summarized previously as reactive, so the first four EC Action Plans over the years 1973 to 1992 have been reactive. The current Environmental Action Plan (1993–1998) is different. It is a proactive programme directed at dealing with the causes of environmental degradation and working towards the goal of sustainable development. It recognizes that the behaviour patterns of producers, consumers, governments and individuals must change if we are to prevent further harm to the environment.

Sustainable development is now an issue on the international political agenda. Predictions suggest that world economic activity may increase fivefold by 2050. Imagine the environmental impact if waste and pollutants increased in proportion to this economic growth, and this will surely happen if the growth merely copies current technology, products, processes and activities. The World Bank, in a report on sustainable development, asserted that development does not imply no growth, but 'doing things differently', and that is a fundamental principle behind integrated pollution management. When asked why something is done a particular way, a common response is 'because we've always done it that way'. In the future, this approach will just convert difficult problems into impossible ones, and so fundamental changes are needed. The President of the World Resources Institute based in Washington DC has suggested a number of transitions that are essential if the root causes of environmental problems are to be addressed.[6] While many of the solutions to underlying causes lie outside the conventional concept of an environmental sector, he doubted that any of the transitions could succeed without the business community's active support and leadership. His list was:

- Demographic transitions: to stabilize the world's population.
- Technology transition: to develop environmentally benign technologies such as low energy paths to production, and manufacturing processes that prevent waste and pollution.

- Economic transition: to reflect the full economic costs and ensure that the best practicable environmental option is cheaper, not more expensive—as is often the case at present.
- Transition in social equity: to share technology and finance dedicated to sustainable development among the rich and poor, since poverty is a great enemy of the environment throughout the world.
- Institutional transitions: to strengthen co-operation and participation among governments, businesses and people.

Here we have a common agenda for business and environmental activists to work together to stress market-based approaches and economic incentives, to introduce new equipment and products, and to recognize that technology is part of the solution and not merely part of the problem. The challenge and opportunity requires:

- Making the environment your issue and not someone else's.
- Moving beyond compliance to leadership, by going beyond standards in developing products for the future.
- Developing proposals for governments to eliminate subsidies and reflect environmental costs.
- Addressing the environmental challenges of the day.
- Being committed to accountability by communicating and being open about your environmental performance.

Perceived Threats

The perceived costs rather than opportunities of environmental protection through reducing waste present major hurdles to overcome in improving attitudes to the need for improving environmental performance. Developing from the introduction to Chapter 1 we can add:

> 'I think the larger companies are more active (on the environment) but smaller ones can't afford it; they are too busy trying to make sure that they don't have to make anyone redundant.'

> 'We're not talking about the environment in our office. The conversation is how are we going to meet our budgets this month, how are we going to survive into next month . . . .'

> 'We will only take action if our profits are threatened.'[7]

The last of these statements provides an indicator to a significant driver, i.e. the commercial pressure, but this has many facets. For example, just as organizations are now accepting quality standards such as BS5750/ISO9000 as adding an air of respectability and meeting the demands of customers, so environmental performance is evolving as an essential component of good business practice. Indeed, environmental quality management may be regarded as merely part of total quality management as we will consider later. However the motivation and justification for (environmental) quality management should be doing the right thing and doing it right; the mark of recognition is merely a bonus. A survey on the awareness of and responses to environmental issues by small firms revealed that the service sector was more concerned than manufacturing and retail, and newer companies were more concerned than older established ones.[8] Significant, however, was the observation that most felt that environmental issues were fundamental rather than transient constraints on organizations, although less than 1 in 10 had carried out an environmental audit or had a policy on suppliers' environmental credentials. This accords with the belief by most that their contribution to pollution was minimal.

Reasons for Inaction: learning from experiences with energy efficiency

Energy efficiency has much in common with environmental protection. Both have the potential of producing benefits including cost-savings to organizations, so why are the opportunities not siezed? Several analyses of the reasons have been produced and from these we can learn. For energy efficiency, constraints preventing uptake of the opportunities by the US Government, the country's largest energy consumer, have been grouped as due to resource constraints, lack of information or insufficient incentive (Table 2.2). There are many parallels with the constraints preventing the adoption of environmental protection measures. However, it is perhaps worth exploring more closely why energy efficiency improvements have often failed to be taken up, despite being 'win-win' investments with significant benefits, particularly financial.

Little can be done about lack of capital as a reason for failure to act on energy inefficiency, although many improvements require little financial investment. More fundamental, perhaps, is the failure to take a long-term view and to associate costs with benefits. Consider the capital and revenue expenditure in an organization. We can break these headings down further as shown in Figure 2.2.

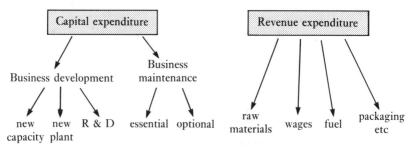

Figure 2.2   Breakdown of capital and revenue expenditure in an organization

Table 2.2 Constraints preventing improved energy efficiency by the US Government. (Adapted from R. Roy, 'Energy Efficiency in the Federal Government: Government by Good Example', in *Power Generation, Energy Management and Environmental Sourcebook*, M. Jackson (Ed.), Fairmont Press Inc., Lilburn GA, distributed by Prentice Hall, 1992)

Resources	Information	Lack of incentives
Priorities favour other needs. Energy efficiency is not central to mission, it is a small cost component of the total budget, and senior managers have little interest in it.	Opportunities have not been systematically examined.	Financial benefits do not accrue to those saving energy. Energy costs are readily accepted as a budget item.
Initial capital spending is a deterrent.	Technical and economic performance is uncertain: Does the technology work? Will the next version be better? No information from monitoring or from similar organizations.	Procurement often favours the status quo, and change is impeded by complex administration systems.
Personnel are needed—there may be no co-ordinator.	Energy-use decisions are made by many individuals, widely dispersed.	
	Co-ordinated efforts are needed. There is little training for the diverse individuals	

Expenditure on environmental improvements (which include energy efficiency) has traditionally been an optional business expense to maintain business activity, with the benefits appearing under a fuel revenue heading. An interesting comparison may be drawn between materials and energy resources here. Despite the relative inaction to improve energy efficiency by introducing conservation measures, data on the improvements in materials use by organizations are still less well documented. This is because traditionally there has been nothing like the same level of concern given to materials supply and use as for energy. This previous lack of emphasis on materials use is remarkable, since materials often constitute a greater part of the total cost of a product than energy, and just as an organization is sensitive to energy supply interruptions, it equally cannot operate without its raw materials.

Particularly for the small business community, health and legislation are principal drivers to push forward on environmental matters, but there are major barriers. A study for Directorate General XI of the Commission of the European Union identified a range of constraints limiting the implementation of environmental technology.[9] The reasons for failing to act included:

- Political and economic issues.
- Environmental policies: lack of legal pressure.

- Legal requirements: changing standards.
- Relevance to core business: organizations may produce waste, but they do not regard themselves as waste managers.
- Risks to core business: reluctance to implement change in process, fearing the expense and perception of risk to business.
- Economics: adverse economic conditions discourage any capital investment.
- Technology transfer issues.
- Access to information: lack of knowledge.
- Confidence: lack of confidence that technology is economically and technically feasible for them.
- Independence: lack of independent advice relevant to specific needs.
- Resources.
- Capabilities: lack of technical expertise for implementation
- Costs: lack of capital to invest.
- Training: low awareness of environmental issues.

Overlaps with the constraints in Table 2.2 are clear, and many of the barriers identified in this survey showed a marked need for greater communication, ranging from raising environmental awareness to detailed technical training and technology transfer issues. Awareness of the general public has been raised to the extent that commercial pressures are an important driver for improved environmental performance. So too is the impact of the supply chain, with business customers having greater expectations of their suppliers, although a legal threat of extended liabilities plays an important part here. The force of regulation appears to be one essential driver for improved environmental performance. This can provide a climate for change which is then implemented more dynamically by economic and commercial pressures.

The Roles of Regulation and Economics

Violations of environmental law carry increasingly severe penalties in addition to the financial costs of cleaning up pollution and accounting for the loss of goodwill. In the US between 1983 and 1990, the Justice Department indicted over 500 individuals and 240 organizations for offences under environmental legislation. The chairman of one major engineering company based in the UK is reported to have told senior managers that it would be unacceptable if he saw unfavourable reports of the company's environmental performance in the newspapers, nor did he want thousands of pounds of profits to be lost in fines for pollution.

In economic terms, costs are clear. They reflect the resources which have to be allocated to a particular activity or technology. Changes in costs over time due to inflation may be accounted for by normal accounting practices.

Discounting, for example, is a reflection of the human tendency to prefer something now rather than in the future. Costs and benefits in the future are reduced by a fixed percentage (the discount rate) for each year in the future to derive an equivalent present value after correction for inflation. As small differences in discount rate become very important over long time periods, the present value of a cost or benefit at a 2 per cent discount rate is reduced by a third over a 20-year period. Longer time periods produce even greater reductions, and environmental issues such as those from carbon dioxide or CFCs released today may have implications a century ahead. Discounting over long periods raises the need for a culture change among those familiar with 2-year payback considerations, and also prompts ethical questions about the balance between generations. Should future generations be given less consideration in terms of their share of natural resources than ourselves?

Nevertheless, the idea that economic growth and environmental protection can be compatible is captured in the previously introduced concept of 'sustainable development'. Definitions of this concept of sustainable development differ. Some argue that it implies that 'a given stock of resources—trees, soil quality, water, etc.—should not decline'. Others suggest that 'as development proceeds, the composition of the underlying asset base changes' and 'a decline in stock levels on its own is not a reason for concern'. The World Bank in its report on Development and the Environment argues that there is no linear relationship between economic activity and environmental damage. In fact some pollutant emissions have declined with development, although this is not the case for municipal waste and carbon dioxide, which have grown with income. The World Bank suggests that 'the key to growing sustainably is not to produce less but produce differently', and this is an important message on integrated pollution management.

To many, the first resource linked to sustainable development is energy, and the economic benefits of efficient energy use have been widely promoted. Yet there is much evidence that despite short-term payback, much is not done that could be done. Often scarce management resources, lack of information and competition with bids ostensibly more central to an organization's activities are excuses for lack of action on energy efficiency improvements, as summarized in Table 2.2. There are clear parallels with environmental management, but the growing tide of public pressure and legal requirements will have a continual and significant effect. Another parallel may be drawn with health and safety legislation, which has brought about major changes in organizations through strong enforcement. Safety issues are not specifically part of IPM, but IPM must recognize the overriding requirement for meeting safety legislation in spirit and to the letter. Indeed, the impact of safety regulation on organizations needs little comment. Health, safety and environmental management are integrated in some organizations, and this growing trend has much to commend it. Rather than having management systems for different issues, a single management system applies to all, which simplifies documentation and the burden on managers.

Incentives for improving the efficiency in the use of materials and energy are now enhanced by environmental concerns. The legal constraints remove the optional or discretionary element of improving performance by making efficiency improvements an integral part of pollution prevention, while the increasing costs of dealing with waste disposal draw attention to the amounts of waste. An instructive parallel can be drawn here with water management in an organization. There are many similarities to the management of energy resources, with the important difference that organizations pay disposal costs on the basis of amount of resource purchased, so cutting down the amount you use cuts your costs twice. An example of this comes from British Rail. The annual water costs mainly associated with train washing at one of its depots were about £70 000, with an additional effluent bill of £60 000. Recycling of water for bodywork cleaning was estimated to be worth £60 000 per year, with associated benefits accruing to the environment.

Problems for financial accounting relate to assigning costs to environmental effects which may be extremely diverse. Should the cost of a litre of petrol for transportation costs include an allowance for the environmental problems such as those caused by the significant emissions of nitrogen oxides, which contribute to acid deposition and ozone pollution at ground level? Putting prices on effects such as reduced crop yield, forest damage and human health effects has been done to a limited extent, but such values are more difficult to comprehend than material values. When we include long-term effects such as depletion of ozone in the upper atmosphere, in terms of our limited lifespan, the effect is irreversible: how do we put a value on that?

We will limit our consideration to more mundane costs. Some of the costs of imperfect environmental management in its widest sense are illustrated by legal penalties. For example, during 1990, ICI received a £100 000 fine after two staff were killed by an explosion that occurred two years previously. Another incident in March 1989 was reported as resulting in a fine of £250 000. Shell Transport and Trading Co was fined £1 million in February 1990 after 156 tonnes of crude oil spilled from a fractured pipeline into the River Mersey. Added to this were the legal costs and the costs of ensuring that similar problems do not occur elsewhere, which probably make the fine relatively insignificant by comparison. Both companies have strong environmental programmes, but it is clear that they do not guarantee that incidents will never occur. A prosecution of Yorkshire Water by the National Rivers Authority (NRA) introduced a different dimension of legal constraints. A spillage of raw sewage from a storm overflow into a stream occurred as a result of maintenance work by contractors. In fining the company £75 000 plus costs, the judge concluded that Yorkshire Water had the choice of supervising its contractors properly to ensure that they acted correctly, or of accepting the blame, and the fine, when things went wrong.[10] The implications for businesses to take serious note of environmental issues through the customer/supplier chain are clear. Yet another development occurred in March 1993. The first prosecution under EPA1990 led to a fine of £1650 with costs of £2000 for failing to seek and obtain an authorization to operate a process using a prescribed substance. Perhaps this may be considered a relatively small fine, but it represents the start of another tightening constraint on organizations. Some organizations escape from their liability to pay for environmental damage caused by their activities, as the example in Chapter 8, Section 1 illustrates, but rulings that undermine the 'polluter pays principle', described below, cannot be guaranteed in the future.

The polluter pays principle

The text of the Organization for Economic Co-operation and Development (OECD) 1972 definition reads:

> Environmental resources are in general limited and their use in production and consumption activities may lead to their deterioration. When the cost of this deterioration is not adequately taken into account in the price system, the market fails to reflect the scarcity of such resources both at the national and international levels. Public measures are thus necessary to reduce pollution and to reach a better allocation of resources by ensuring that the prices of goods depending on the quality and/or quantity of environmental resources reflect more closely their relative scarcity and that economic agents concerned react accordingly.
>
> In many circumstances, in order to ensure that the environment is in an acceptable state, the reduction of pollution beyond a certain level will not be practical or even necessary in view of the costs involved.
>
> The principle to be used for allocating costs of pollution prevention and control measures to encourage rational use of scarce environmental resources and to avoid distortions in international trade and investment is the so-called 'Polluter Pays Principle'. This principle means that the polluter should bear the expenses of carrying out the above mentioned measures decided by public authorities to ensure that the environment is in an acceptable state. In other words, the cost of goods and services which cause pollution in production and/or consumption. Such measures should not be accompanied by subsidies that would create significant distortions in international trade and investment. The principle should be an objective of Member countries . . .

Fines are, perhaps, manifestations of the polluter pays principle that first spring to mind. Other consequences of the principle appear in various guises. One example in the UK is the introduction of cost recovery charging which applies to IPC, to local authority air pollution control, and to the NRA controls on water pollution. As an illustration of this, under EPA1990, HMIP is obliged to recover all of its direct regulatory costs from industry by charging for IPC applications, and by levying an annual subsistence charge. Such charges are straightforward, but the imponderables in assessing environmental costs present difficulties. Criteria such as BATNEEC (Best Available Techniques Not Entailing Excessive Costs) circumvent the difficulties. Legal instruments such as BATNEEC include costs in terms of requiring environmental improvements 'not entailing excessive costs'. In the developing EU policy of IPPC (Integrated Pollution Prevention and Control), BAT encompasses the cost item in the 'available techniques', being dependent upon costs. There can be no place, however, for cultures based on other acronyms such as CATNIP (Cheapest Available Technology Not Involving Prosecution). Indeed, what may be legally permitted now, may present liabilities in the future, and contaminated land is a classic example of this. Once again, the long-term vision is called for, together with preparedness for an uncertain future.

Energy prices are important in the context of both resource consumption and pollution production. Energy demand can respond quite strongly to price changes, but many countries subsidize energy and so encourage over-consumption. In the context of combatting global warming, the main aim is to limit carbon dioxide emissions, and a way of dealing with this is to tax carbon rather than energy activities themselves. Carbon-based fuels would be taxed in proportion to their carbon content (approximately in the ratio $100 : 77 : 56$ for coal:oil:gas, respectively). If carbon taxes are introduced they would provide incentives to reduce waste and to switch to lower carbon-content fuels, and clearly represent an application of the polluter pays principle.

Long-term financial liability

Few pieces of legislation can have created more concern to businesses than the so-called 'Superfund' Act in the USA. This legislation, formally called the Comprehensive Environmental Response Compensation and Liability Act (CERCLA), was introduced in 1980 and perhaps represents the ultimate in application of the polluter pays principle. Numerous estimates on the costs of restoration of contaminated sites have appeared, but a general trend is apparent. One summary[11] suggests that in summer 1991 the restoration costs were in the range $70–250 billion, but by November of that year the cost estimate had risen to $420 billion. Just one month later, the estimate was $750 billion. This growth is not surprising when additional contaminated sites continue to be identified, and the average Superfund site restoration costs are in the range $30–50 million. Such costs encourage organizations to find ways to share liability, with the ultimate burden often falling on the insurance industry.

It is no surprise, therefore, that the financial sector is increasingly looking closely at future risks. In the UK, plans for a register of land subjected to potential contaminating uses were proposed under provisions of the Environmental Protection Act 1990, but were withdrawn. The difficulties of tackling the problems of historic pollution will not go away, however, for subsequent UK proposals suggest that current owners of land should be liable for pollution on that land. Wider European initiatives are possible in the future in the guise of a Directive on Civil Liability for Damage Caused by Waste. The implications of such legislation are revolutionary in Europe. Holding producers of any waste liable for any damage it causes irrespective of fault on their part, or in their absence treating waste contractors as deemed producers, reflects much of Superfund. The principle of 'joint and several' liability with banks having lent money to the waste producers, or their insurers, sharing the liability explains the growing interest of the financial sector in environmental issues. Effectively the banks and insurance companies are likely to become aiders and abetters in the regulatory system, enforcing companies to raise their environmental standards. However this legal area develops, it is a significant spur towards waste minimization, the heart of any integrated pollution management system.

Individual liability

We have already given examples of how responsibility for poor environmental performance depends on the actions of individuals, and more will be given later. Increasing pressure is falling on managers to shoulder the burden of poor environmental performance. An example of allocating responsibility with accountability comes from the Netherlands. The Dutch Government started developing its sustainable development strategy in 1990, and resolved to concentrate on sectors which made the greatest contributions to environmental problems in the country. One element of the national environmental policy is to encourage an organization to take responsibility for the environment in which it is situated. This approach attempts to balance the environmental and economic aspects of the activities involved against the sensitivity of the locality to environmental damage. Clear statements from government provide industry with an agenda of what is expected, and the onus is on the organization to be aware of its responsibilities, change its behaviour and make the environment an integral part of the daily operations of the firm. This 'deregulation' stimulates greater responsibility on the part of organizations for the environmental consequences of their actions, but is also part of a steering approach that recognizes that, over time, existing regulations can become counter-productive. It also allows for the fact that enforcement can be the weakest link in the regulatory chain. In this system, responsibility is translated into a system of internal enforcement. Differentiated systems of environmental management have evolved according to business activities, but the focus is on an environmental audit approach. Environmental management systems have developed further, and we will address these performance measurements in later chapters.

Underpinning the individual responsibility of organizations there is a responsibility of each and every one of us to participate in pollution prevention.

Individuals tend to imagine that individual response is insignificant and ineffective, but environmental protection is the sum of individual human actions. Many of the major pollution incidents of the past have been linked with human action (or inaction). A public displaying guilt over lack of action may assuage that guilt by placing blame on business for large scale damage, and on government for soft policies. However studies, again from the Netherlands, illustrate the direct and significant contribution that households make to environmental problems. Householders use over 30 per cent more water than industry, generate waste at one of the highest rates in Europe and have a lifestyle that encourages intensive livestock farming with its associated waste management and pollution problems. Individuals must be encouraged to recognize their responsibilities for environmental harm and their role in dealing with the problems. Organizations must demonstrate their concern for the environment to their employees and the public, and generate an attitude that good environmental practice at work and in daily life have much in common. Enlisting the help of energy and water utilities, industry groups, trade unions and pressure groups is aimed at influencing changes in lifestyles. Cultivating this good practice at work and at home is part of a company's environmental management system as we will describe later.

The Rise of Public Concern and Peer Group Pressure: Environment is News!

Abraham Lincoln summarized the importance of public opinion:

> 'Public sentiment is everything. With [it], nothing can fail, without it nothing can succeed; consequently he who moulds public sentiment goes deeper than he who enacts statutes and decisions. He makes statutes and decisions possible or impossible.'[12]

Throughout the latter half of the twentieth century, there has been a steady growth in environmental concerns despite the other distractions in public opinion through a variety of political and economic vicissitudes. Local environmental issues always generate interest and concern, with proposed developments often facing the NIMBY (Not In My Back Yard) syndrome. Better information systems through a variety of media and several environmental disasters of natural and human origin have heightened awareness of wider environmental issues and potential risks to our well-being. Public opinion polls in various countries suggest concern but the willingness to act through purchasing power and other means is not always forthcoming. The perceived magnitude of global issues may indicate that local action is futile, although the solutions start locally, as Agenda 21 programmes indicate.

Public attitudes in the UK are summarized in *The UK Environment*,[13] based on various opinion polls. In the 1970s the proportion of people surveyed who indicated environmental or pollution issues as being the major issue fluctuated between 1 and 7 per cent, and it was not until 1988 that the environment was ranked sufficiently highly to merit its separate consideration from other concerns. The peak of concern occurred in July 1989, when some 35 per cent of the sampled population said that the environment was the most or one of the most important issues. This sampling period corresponded with the European elections and influences on environmental issues from Europe have always been strong. Normally, however, media coverage highlights certain issues at the expense of others, and so there is a continuous variation in awareness and concern. By 1993 public concern about pollution and the environment remained high, being ranked third after unemployment and health/social services, and this was despite four years of recession. There was also widespread support for application of the polluter pays principle.[14] Another European-wide survey in 1988 revealed that throughout the EC some 74 per cent of the population thought that pollution and environmental damage was an urgent and immediate problem, whereas in the UK this view was held by 67 per cent. Moreover, in the UK 25 per cent considered environmental pollution was a problem for the future, while only 20 per cent held this view throughout the EC.

Public awareness

Evidence suggests that while environmental concern appears widespread and growing, the understanding of many issues is poor. This view is echoed in market research carried out for the Open University's environmental education and training programme,[7] which revealed a number of significant findings. For example, while there was concern about the business community's neglect of environmental issues, employees (i.e. a sector of the public) were not pressurizing business to take action. Despite the growth in public concern, there appears still to be a great deal of confusion in the general public and it is clear that while the media influence raises awareness, and even 'makes you feel guilty', it often does little to dispel uncertainty and scepticism.

Respondents in the survey said:

'The pocket comes first in most people's minds. I know the environment is important but at the moment, the [economic] climate being as it is, the pocket comes first.'

'. . . but they've been telling us about it for umpteen years, we have been wasting things, water, more and more.'

'The thing with most people is that, yes, they are interested, yes they would like it done, as long as they are not the ones who have to go and do it . . .'

suggesting that positive leadership and demonstration of commitment is essential, even to the extent of addressing issues which by some criteria are of lesser importance. The Pareto concept is named after Pareto, a nineteenth century Italian economist, who found that relatively few people owned a large share of wealth. This concept suggests that 80 per cent of problems result from 20 per cent of the causes. A key step to improving performance is to deal with the important 20 per cent, but should you ignore the 80 per cent of less important environmental issues?

Our view is that you cannot afford to ignore issues that may have a relatively minor impact in themselves. For example, switching off a single light in your office may have relatively little impact on global warming, but the integral of everyone acting similarly will have significant impact. Switching off your light may help motivate others. Likewise, launching an environmental management programme focusing on major process activities in an organization may fail if issues such as proliferation of paper are not addressed. This is an important aspect of communication we will return to later.

We indicated some differences in public opinion between countries earlier, but environmental issues and crises do not abide by our artificial borders and the barriers of the seas and mountains. Organizations must manage environmental affairs on an international stage, and recognize the differences in cultures, attitudes and expectations of various countries. International communications are now so swift through the media of satellite and other networks that an event in one country quickly comes under the spotlight on the other side of the earth. National issues are consequently transforming into global ones, both on the political and legislative agendas as well as on the organizational agenda. The power of public opinion must never be underestimated. Reputations your organization spent years building can be destroyed in a moment. Similar pressures apply to governments, and international disapproval can produce action. The reputation of being 'the dirty man of Europe' was influential in making Britain agree to cease dumping of sewage sludge in the North Sea, and similar peer pressure has been applied to the USA in relation to its production of gases contributing to global warming.

The younger generation

It would be remiss if we concluded this section on public pressures without reference to children. There has been a great deal of success in environmental education in schools, which has made children more aware of the threats to their environment from an early age; recognizing that they have a personal interest in a long-term future. Children often inform and increasingly are pushing their parents in their purchasing patterns.

'When my daughter comes to the supermarket with me, she always gets me to buy the environmentally friendly products. She is always telling me what to buy and when she is with me I feel a little bit guilty. So I do put them in the trolley. But normally it is the cost which stops me.'[7]

Children expect a proactive response from industry to address environmental issues, with government pressure acting as necessary.[15] As future consumers their knowledge may grow ahead of that of producers, who will have to overcome a public increasingly cynical about product claims.

Market Pressures

The Advisory Committee on Business and the Environment (ACBE) was set up as a UK Government initiative early in 1991. The first report of the committee called for stronger policies on energy efficiency and resource recycling. Only by making great changes in these areas can targets such as cutting emissions of 'greenhouse gases' be achieved and business opportunities siezed to match the developments of our international competitors.

At the 1990 conference of the Confederation of British Industry (CBI), the Secretary of State for the Environment stated that:

'Poor environmental performance is likely to be a sign of poor market performance. The most profitable companies are often the cleanest.'

At the same forum, Professor David Bellamy proposed 10 guidelines for business, including the following:

- 'Cradle-to-grave' audits of all company products or services
- Link environmental plans with quality programmes
- Adopt an environmentally sensitive approach to new products/processes

He also proposed that anything entering a production system for any purpose should end as part of a saleable or reusable by-product. Around the same time, the so-called 'Valdez Principles' were produced by a coalition of US fund managers and environmentalists: the Coalition for Environmentally Responsible Economies (CERES). The principles were named after the Exxon Valdez supertanker which ran aground off the coast of Alaska in March 1989. The Exxon Corporation spent over $2 billion in clean-up costs during the following two years, with more subsequently. While regarded as more symbolic than practical, the Valdez Principles, now known as the CERES Principles, raised awareness and set a framework for shareholder activism (Table 2.3).

It will be apparent from the CERES Principles that selling the case for good environmental management is essential, and this involves informing not just personnel at all levels in the organization, but also stakeholders and the general public. These aspects will be considered further in Chapter 7. Unfortunately the principles have not found widespread favour among shareholders. Exxon stated that the Valdez Principles 'fail to recognize the need to balance environ-

Table 2.3 The CERES Principles

Protection of the biosphere	Minimize and seek to eliminate release of pollutants causing damage to the air, water, or earth or its inhabitants. Safeguard habitats in rivers, lakes, wetlands, coastal zones and oceans, and minimize contributing to the greenhouse effect, depletion of the ozone layer, acid rain, or smog.
Sustainable use of natural resources	Make sustainable use of natural resources, such as water, soils and forests. Conserve non-renewable natural resources through efficient use and careful planning. Protect wildlife habitat, open spaces, and wilderness while preserving biodiversity.
Reduction and disposal of wastes	Minimize creation of waste, especially hazardous waste, and whenever possible recycle materials. Dispose of waste by safe and responsible methods.
Wise use of energy	Make every effort to use environmentally safe and sustainable energy sources. Invest in improved energy efficiency and conservation in our operations. Maximize energy efficiency of products we produce or sell.
Risk reduction	Minimize environmental health and safety risks to employees and communities in which we operate by employing safe technologies and operating procedures and by being constantly prepared for emergencies.
Marketing of safe products and services	Sell products or services that minimize environmental impacts and are safe as consumers use them. Inform consumers of environmental impacts of products or services.
Damage compensation	Take responsibility for harm we cause to the environment by making every effort to fully restore the environment and compensate persons adversely effected.
Disclosure	Disclose to employees and the public incidents relating to operations that cause environmental harm or pose health and safety hazards. Disclose potential environmental, health or safety hazards posed by operations and take no action against employees who report conditions that create a danger to the environment or pose health and safety hazards.
Environmental directors and managers	Commit management resources to implement these principles, to monitor and report on implementation, and to sustain a process to ensure that the board and chief executive officer are kept informed of, and are fully responsible for, environmental matters. Establish a committee of the board with responsibility for environmental affairs. Have one board member qualified to represent environmental interests.
Assessment and annual audit	Conduct and make public an annual self-evaluation of progress in implementing these principles and in complying with all applicable laws and regulations throughout worldwide operations. Work towards timely creation of independent environmental audit procedures completed annually and made available to the public.

mental protection with a healthy economy and an adequate energy supply', favouring instead principles such as the chemical industries' 'Responsible Care' programme (see Chapter 3). Exxon nevertheless created an Environment and Safety Department under the leadership of a vice-president reporting directly to the president of the company. A progress report on the environment was also published in 1991, while a public issues committee of the board was established to review company policies, programmes and practices as they relate to public issues.

Further standards and guidelines have been developed. For example, the Maquiladora Standards of Conduct developed by a group of over 60 religious, environmental, community and other groups concern not just environmental but also health and safety and labour practices in targeted companies. Emphasizing Mexican operations, this is a further illustration of the global concern of stakeholders in environmental issues.

Of course, developments elsewhere have moved on apace. Many organizations have produced environmental policies, programmes and corporate structures, while external pressures are also playing a part. These pressures may be legislative, such as through the Integrated Pollution Control (IPC) philosophy in the UK Environmental Protection Act (1990), similar approaches in other European countries and the emerging Integrated Pollution Prevention and Control (IPPC) philosophy being developed in the EU. Other pressures include the EU Regulation on the Eco Management and Audit Scheme (EMAS) and the British Standard on Environmental Management Systems (BS7750), while the power of commercial pressures through the supply chain must not be underestimated. We have also described previously the emergence of the concept of sustainable development and the pivotal role of environmental protection emphasized in the 1987 report, *Our Common Future* (Brundtland Commission).

To help businesses around the world improve their environmental performance, in 1991 the International Chamber of Commerce (ICC) drew together representatives of business to create a Business Charter for Sustainable Development, which comprises 16 principles (Table 2.4).

Many similarities between the ICC Principles and the CERES Principles will be noticed, including the explicit communication concepts of reporting and education as set out in Principles 4, 7, 11, 12, 13, 14, 15 and 16. The role of the supply chain and the resulting commercial pressures are also evident from Principle 11, while throughout there is an assumption that environmental management applies equally to manufacturing and to service sector organizations. The rising tide of legal obligations also shows many common features with these principles.

Co-operation: industry and government

Experience has shown that the prerequisite to environmental success is government commitment with the co-operation of independent sectors of business in setting priorities and making (often difficult) choices from what may be conflicting options. The enthusiasm of non-governmental organizations can

Table 2.4   The ICC Business Charter for Sustainable Development: principles for environmental management (Source: *European Environment*, vol. 1, part 4, 1991)

1	Corporate priority	To recognize environmental* management as among the highest corporate priorities and as a key determinant to sustainable development; to establish policies, programmes and practices for conducting operations in an environmentally sound manner.
2	Integrated management	To integrate these policies, programmes and practices fully into each business as an essential element of management in all its functions.
3	Process of improvement	To continue to improve corporate policies, programmes and environmental performance, taking into account technical developments, scientific understanding, consumer needs and community expectations, with legal regulations as a starting point; and to apply the same environmental criteria internationally.
4	Employee education	To educate train and motivate employees to conduct their activities in an environmentally responsible manner.
5	Prior assessment	To assess environmental impacts before starting a new activity or project and before decommissioning a facility or leaving a site.
6	Products and services	To develop and provide products or services that have no undue environmental impact and are safe in their intended use, that are efficient in their consumption of energy and natural resources, and that can be recycled, reused or disposed of safely.
7	Customer advice	To advise, and where relevant educate, customers, distributors and the public in the safe use, transportation, storage and disposal of products provided; and to apply similar considerations to the provision of services.
8	Facilities and operations	To develop, design and operate facilities and conduct activities taking into consideration the efficient use of energy and materials, the sustainable use of renewable resources, the minimization of adverse environmental impact and waste generation, and the safe and responsible disposal of residual waste.
9	Research	To conduct or support research on the environmental impacts of raw materials, products, processes, emissions and wastes asssociated with the enterprise and on the means of minimizing such adverse impacts.
10	Precautionary approach	To modify the manufacture, marketing or use of products or services or the conduct of activities, consistent with scientific or technical understanding, to prevent serious or irreversible environmental degradation.
11	Contractors and suppliers	To promote the adoption of these principles by contractors acting on behalf of the enterprise, encouraging and, where appropriate, requiring improvements in their practices to make them consistent with those of the enterprise; and to encourage the wider adoption of these principles by suppliers.
12	Emergency preparedness	To develop and maintain, where significant hazards exist, emergency preparedness plans in conjunction with the emergency service, relevant authorities and the local community, recognizing potential transboundary impacts.

(continued)

Table 2.4 (*Concluded*)

13	Transfer of technology	To contribute to the transfer of environmentally sound technology and management methods throughout the industrial and public sectors.
14	Contributing to the common effort	To contribute to the development of public policy and to business, governmental and intergovernmental programmes and educational initiatives that will enhance environmental awareness and protection.
15	Openness to concerns	To foster openness and dialogue with employees and the public, anticipating and responding to their concerns about the potential hazards and impacts of operations, products, wastes or services, including those of transboundary or global significance.
16	Compliance and reporting	To measure environmental performance; to conduct regular environmental audits and assessments of compliance with company requirements, legal requirements and these principles; and periodically to provide appropriate information to the board of directors, shareholders, employees, the authorities and the public.

* The term environmental in this table also refers to environmentally related aspects of health, safety and product stewardship.

contribute to monitoring implementation, but a major factor involves co-operation and co-ordination of local, regional, national and international efforts. In its second annual environment report published in 1993,[16] ICI plc noted that progress on recycling was 'slower that we would want'. An explanation given for this noted the need for co-operation of many parties: other industries, local and national governments and the consumer. Unfortunately, this degree of co-operation is not always easy to achieve.

National priorities on the environment will inevitably differ and change over time and so will the pressures placed on organizations within those nation states. Early technological development may result in certain forms of pollution increasing and then decreasing as the country becomes wealthier. Problems with untreated sewage or smoke and sulphur dioxide from coal and oil burning still affect the health of many in developing countries as they did in the UK in the nineteenth century and first half of the twentieth century. Statistics show how environmental detriment from these forms of pollution has been reduced over the years, but increasing affluence brings with it new environmental problems. Now we have the pressures from municipal and industrial waste, as well as the secondary pollution generated from motor vehicle emissions. Added to these problems is the less life-threatening, but potentially more environmentally significant, increase in global warming gases. National priorities will also differ according to the provision for other investments. How does one balance reducing poverty or providing for primary health care against regulating for clean air?

Geographical factors can also temper environmental perspectives, as is demonstrated by comparing the potential impact of and attitudes to discharges upwind or upstream, or into a tidal sea or enclosed lake. Much European legislation has been driven by a desire to harmonize standards towards the 'level playing field' and to avoid competitive advantage for a country having low environmental standards. The perceived advantage of lax standards is readily apparent; less so is the claimed advantage of raising standards. Some argue that the more demanding standards in countries such as Germany and Japan have given those countries competitive advantage in the environmental control equipment market. Differences in standards were in conflict with the market policy of the European Union, and resulted in the harmonization highlighted at the beginning of this section. The harmonization is partial, however, for more stringent standards are permitted and exist. Such standards often set the pace for future developments. In 1983, following political pressure, Germany had enacted legislation to control sulphur dioxide emissions from power generating plant by either fitting flue gas desulphurization plant or closing down. Industrial pressure over the impact on electricity prices pressurized the German government to put pressure on other EU members to adopt similar requirements, and the Large Combustion Plant Directive of 1988 was the outcome.

Dealing with existing plant

There will always be conflicts, especially between economic, social and environmental considerations. Old and highly polluting operations may have to continue in operation owing to the great social costs of closure, but large gains can often be achieved by the 'win-win' action of good housekeeping. Attention to maintenance, installing better control systems and improving standards of plant and process management can improve both the economic performance of the organization and lessen the environmental impact of the processes. There is always a role for continuous improvements through these incremental actions, since application of the Best Available Techniques is not always justifiable on these wider considerations. We examine many of these options in later chapters and case studies.

The burden of responsibility

Just as decision-making traditionally takes financial issues into consideration, environmental issues should now become equally part of the corporate culture. An analysis of the evolution of integrated environmental management has related to environmental units within large organizations.[17] The status and function of the environmental unit has evolved to become part of the decision-making structure with an influence on strategy and development within organi-

Table 2.5 Evolution of environmental management units in large organizations

Before 1980	1984–1988	Late 1980s
Small groups mainly reacting to regulatory pressures through producing reports and research, especially toxicological.	Growth in environmental care systems including training and education at all levels in the organization.	Tendency to think strategically about environmental issues in terms of threat and opportunities for the business. Proactive and preventive courses of action gain ground.

zations (Table 2.5). Bringing environmental considerations into strategic planning is important: plan for the unexpected, however improbable it may seem. Consider, for example, an organization abstracting water from a lake in order to dilute an effluent to comply with a discharge consent written in terms of concentrations. How would you address the requirement to cease abstracting in the unusual circumstance that drought conditions occur? The impact on your legal compliance could be devastating.

The evolution of environmental management is well illustrated by the unprecedented increase in the number of environmental managers in British business in the early 1990s. While much of their work still relates to regulatory compliance, pollution prevention through minimizing waste production is a growing work-load, while screening suppliers for good environmental performance is another aspect we will touch on shortly. Increasingly they are becoming co-ordinators, as environmental management becomes integrated into the work of line managers who have the responsibility for control. Often, safety, health and environmental issues are linked (as 'SHE' issues), and the evolution of safety management offers a useful model.

> 'Good health and safety practices become part of the culture of an organization. They have come to be perceived by responsible managers as important aspects of management, not separate from the day-to-day running of the business, but central to it.'
>
> Sir John Cullen, former Chairman of the Health & Safety Commission[18]

For many years health and safety legislation has imposed legal obligations on organizations and on individuals. The threat of liability under environmental law is another pressure on individuals. If you are the environmental manager in an organization, have you considered whether in law you are the person responsible for 'environmental harm'? In practice you may have no 'control' over processes; that may be the responsibility of site management. The board of a public company should formally endorse the environmental policy and objectives so that they know what they are responsible for, and to show that they know the commitments they have made. Directors of a publicly quoted organization are ultimately answerable to their shareholders, in whose hands are the voting rights for elections to the board. In the USA, a director database has been developed to enable shareholders to evaluate directors standing for election based on the environmental record of all the companies on whose boards they have served.[19] As corporate liabilities and the associated costs have escalated, particularly in the USA as a result of Superfund site clean up, shareholders have also exercised another right: that of taking legal action with the effect of transferring a significant part of an organization's environmental liability to its directors and officers.

This approach is spreading, for an offensive by Friends of the Earth warns that prosecutions will be taken against the directors of companies which do not improve their performance in meeting discharge consents.[20] In the UK the legal provision to do this is contained in section 217 of the Water Resources Act 1991, which makes a director or senior officer of a company criminally liable for a pollution offence committed with 'consent or connivance' or 'attributable to any neglect' of that person. This issue of legal liability is a complex one and for specific details on this advice should be sought from your legal advisor or from specialized publications.[21]

Opportunities

Environmentally friendly design and product specification

Integrating environmental assessment and product development may result in long-term financial advantage through what is variously known as 'green design' or 'design for environment'. Marketing, manufacturing and R&D strategies are all part of an integrated system within an organization and environmental considerations should be treated similarly. Products must perform to the customer's needs, and increasingly this involves concern throughout the life cycle of the product or service as we saw from Figure 1.1.

It is not unknown for a company to be notified by a business customer that none of its products must have been manufactured using, say, CFCs by a deadline well in advance of national policy guidelines phasing out such materials, as our third case study (Chapter 8, Section 3) illustrates. This demonstrates the unexpected constraint and challenge posed by the distinction between 'containing' and 'manufactured using'. Indications are that customer orientated divisions of an organization are more likely to have concern for environmental issues and have more advanced environmental management systems in place. They may seek out new production processes or materials to minimize waste and avoid risk of accidents and accept that the technological challenges offer an impetus for innovation.

Pressures from consumer organizations and media coverage together with the value judgements society increasingly makes have contributed to customer demands for environmentally friendly products. The market growth of speciality products such as phosphate-free detergents, the acceptance by customers of recycled products and the demands for environmentally friendly products in the widest sense have had a profound influence on many businesses.

A proactive approach is preferred by some business customers. British Telecom, reportedly the largest private purchaser in the UK (spending around £4000 million each year on equipment, services and materials), integrates environmental factors into its supplier selection processes. Tenders for major contracts must include an assessment of the life cycle impact of goods or services. The environmental impact is fed into the supplier selection process to identify and discriminate against environmentally harmful items.

The Body Shop, a commercially successful, international skin and hair care company selling over 400 products from 700 stores in 41 countries, is driven by the social and environmental implications of everything it does. To ensure that its suppliers exercise the high level of environmental commitment expected of them, The Body Shop has also put in place a formal system of life cycle assessment to establish the environmental credentials of its suppliers. The company is '... outraged that environmental auditing is not yet compulsory in business.'[22] This exemplifies the pressure on suppliers to change how things are made, what materials are used, and to adopt a wider perspective to encompass the whole life cycle from procurement of supplies to customer disposal of products and packaging, etc. However, such a high profile may make an organization vulnerable to adverse media reporting, necessitating impeccable environmental credentials if commercial performance is not to suffer. Another business exerting pressure on its suppliers is the retailer B & Q, which uses a 40-page questionnaire to assess its suppliers, and assigns them a score according to their performance against criteria specified in Table 2.6.

The environment and corporate policy

Elsewhere in organizations the integration of environmental considerations may be more subtle, such as in marketing and sales. We have seen that small organizations are unlikely to have the personnel or financial resources to support an environmental unit or co-ordinator, and consequently they often depend on the expertise of their larger suppliers. By designing products that solve customers' environmental problems and by providing technical support, the customers are themselves better able to meet environmental regulations, while the supplier offers added value to its products and maintains business.

Financial benefits may accompany good environmental practice, but clearly are not the sole justification for good environmental performance and will not be until financial values are placed on the 'free' or uncosted resources of the environment. However, financial benefits can be a considerable bonus with relatively short-term payback, whereas the environmental benefits have more distant horizons.

Table 2.6   Supplier grading applied by the retailer B&Q

Grading	Features of supplier action
A	Has comprehensive environmental management programme
	Takes proactive stance on environmental issues
	Offers business opportunities
B	Has an environmental policy
	Has identified all major issues relevant to company and recognizes role in managing them
	May offer business opportunities
C	Policy is only a mission statement which does not demonstrate real awareness
	Action taken is not comprehensive and reactive
	No real targets or action plans
D	Reaction justifies *status quo*
	No policy and no action
	Performance should be improved
E	Supplier exposes customer to severe liability
	Action essential if business links to be maintained
F	Fail

The view is sometimes expressed that tackling environmental issues is little more than a shallow, expensive, public relations exercise. Some organizations may indeed do it with this motivation, but any benefits are short-lived sales gains, and not sustained improvement in company performance. Consequently, much depends on the backing and commitment of senior management, and the involvement of all staff. These are issues that will be developed further in Chapter 7, but given these essential components, we will demonstrate that improving environmental performance has positive long-term benefits. There is no magic about environmental audits, life cycle analysis and other techniques of environmental management; they are merely management tools, but achieving the benefits demands action on their findings. If the recommendations of a thorough audit are adopted, the real benefits it can bring include improved efficiency, less waste of materials, lower energy bills, reduced discharges to the environment, improved market share through market differentiation, and an increased ability to recruit and retain staff.

Total quality management and the environment

Good environmental management is part of total quality management, and an organization with effective quality systems in place should minimize problems and may not require environmental inspection so frequently as an organization without such systems. Proven good environmental management systems supported by audit data may be demanded before you can secure a bank loan, may be required by your customers before they will buy from you and by investors before they will invest in you. In the past, public liability insurance policies normally did not exclude pollution, and underwriting potential claims presents major problems in the future. Insurers are therefore likely to seek audit data before taking new risks. Few can now believe that having a good environmental performance is an optional extra; what was once regarded as offering a market advantage is becoming a prerequisite to entering the market-place.

Conclusions

The beginning of this decade brought the concept of integrated pollution control into legislation. The early years of the decade also demonstrated that environmental management is an integral part of the management system of all organizations. Drucker[23] notes that the first responsibility of a profession was spelled out clearly in ancient Greece, some 2500 years ago, in the Hippocratic Oath. *Primum non nocere*: 'above all, not knowingly to do harm' is an equally valid basic rule for the ethics of any professional, whether in medicine, engineering or management. In the context of integrated pollution management we need to consider ways of not causing harm to the environment.

All organizations exist to provide something for society, and so have to exist in society. They exist in communities, carry out their activities in a social setting and also employ people to carry out those activities. These interactions are inescapable as are the interactions of society with the wider environmental system. Analysing the interactions, identifying options for improvements, implementing the best option and maintaining performance are some of the techniques we have to consider. Human factors play an important part in environmental issues, and we all have a role in minimizing harm to the environment. We all have a vested interest in the future whether through our own lives or those of our descendants. We also have a significant role in improving the environmental performance of organizations whether as shareholders, employers, employees or customers.

Awareness of environmental issues has increased in recent years, and with the idea of Agenda 21 in mind, we have a plausible view back from that century:[24]

'The 21st Century will look back on the industrial pollution and accidents of the 20th Century with the same level of antipathy that we in the 20th Century view the slavery and child labour practices of the 19th Century.'

Practical Points for Action

- Plan ahead: include environmental issues in strategic planning.
- Prepare for the unexpected.

- Look for the opportunities rather than threats in environmental developments.
- Consider integrating environmental considerations into the normal management system of your organization.
- Recognize the costs of poor environmental performance.
- Remember that 'the key to growing sustainably is not to produce less but produce differently'.
- Managers must:
  Keep up to date.
  Learn about new developments from others: competitors, customers, suppliers, trade journals, networks etc.
  Monitor current technology processes: watch for new concerns, stress factors that may influence performance, and potential health aspects.
  Watch effects of technology on management supervision structure.
  Get enthusiasts to lead: high commitment is essential.
  Introduce technological change in existing location: people dislike multiple changes.
  Sell new systems: persuade operators to change, explain benefits, use all possible ways to promote change.
  Provide a role model by personal action.
- Avoid:
  Assuming that technology remains as effective as when installed.
  Taking the view that there will be no further change.
  Assuming that others see the advantages.
  Introducing too much change at once.
  Secrecy about technology: people like to know, to participate and to contribute.
  Political arguments about the best technology: it creates later difficulties.

References

1   Department of Trade and Industry, *Overseas Trade*, March 1994.
2   Touche Ross Europe Services, 'European Management Attitudes to Environmental Issues', 1990.
3   David Bellamy Associates, 'Industry Goes Green', 1991.
4   United Nations Commission on Environment and Development, *Our Common Future*, Oxford University Press, Oxford, 1987.
5   The Conservation Foundation, 'The Road from Rio', 1993.
6   J. G. Speth, 'The Environmental Agenda for Leaders', *Directors & Boards*, vol. 15, no. 4, 1991, 5–8.
7   Dr J. Citron of Dialog, 'Investigation of the Barriers, Drivers and Needs in Environmental Education & Training', A report on qualitative research prepared for the OU Environmental Education and Training Programme, June 1993.
8   Cranfield Institute, 'How Green are Small Companies?', 1990.

9   M. Sharpe, 'The Network for Environmental Technology Transfer: Serving Europe's Information Needs', *Environmental Pollution 1, ICEP-1, Proceedings*, vol. 1, Inderscience, Geneva, 1991, 461–469.

10 '£75 000 "buck" Stops with Yorkshire Water after Contractor Error', ENDS Report 221, June 1993, 44.

11 D. T. Reed, I. R. Tasker, J. C. Cunnane, and G. F. Vandegrift, 'Environmental Restoration and Separation Science', in *Environmental Remediation*, G. F. Vandegrift, D. T. Reed, and I. R. Tasker (Eds), ACS Symposium Series 509, American Chemical Society, Washington DC, 1992, 3.

12 J. R. Hall, 'In the Jaws of a Crisis', *Directors & Boards*, vol. 15, no. 4, 1991, 17.

13 Department of the Environment, *The UK Environment*, HMSO, London, 1992.

14 *Digest of Environmental Protection & Water Statistics*, no. 16, HMSO, London, 1994.

15 British Telecom, 'Young Eyes: children's visions of the future environment', Survey by Henley Management Centre for British Telecom.

16 Environmental Performance, 1993, ICI plc, 9 Millbank, London.

17 P. Groenewegen, and P. Vergragt, 'Environmental Issues as Threats and Opportunities for Technological Innovation', *Technology Analysis & Strategic Management*, vol. 3, no. 1, 43–55.

18 Sir John Cullen, 'Health & Safety: A Burden on Business?', Process Safety & Environmental Protection, *Transactions of the Institute of Chemical Engineers Part B*, vol. 72, February 1994, 3–9.

19 N. Minow, and M. Deal, 'The Shareholders' Green Focus', *Directors & Boards*, vol. 15, no. 4, 1991, 35–39.

20 ENDS Report 221, June 1993, 8.

21 S. Tromans and G. Irvine, *Directors in the Dock: Personal Liability Under Environmental Law*, Technical Communications (Publishing) Ltd, Letchworth, 1994.

22 Body Shop International plc, *The Green Book*, West Sussex, England, May 1992.

23 P. F. Drucker, *Management*, an abridged and revised version of *Management: Tasks, Responsibilities, Practices*, Pan Business Management, London, 1979.

24 B. C. Ball, T. H. Lee, and R. D. Tabors, 'Energy Systems for the 21st Century', *International Journal of Global Energy Systems*, vol. 1, 1989.

3

Understanding Environmental Performance

Before you can consider how the environmental performance of your organization can be improved it is essential to assess the current performance. The magnitude of the problem will be different if you are a large multinational company compared with, say, a small garage or store. However, the steps in the analysis of the current position will be much the same.

In the first instance it can be useful to invite someone not directly involved with the plant concerned to look at it objectively and give you some initial reactions. Perhaps your partner could call in and spend an hour or two just strolling around. This could identify simple matters like lights or machines left on unnecessarily, high energy bulbs being used when low energy alternatives are available, oil films on puddles in the loading/unloading area, windows and doors left open when heating is on, smells of solvent or chemicals in work areas perhaps indicating inadequate containment, paper being copied or typed on one side only, and waste not being adequately segregated.

These may seem trivial matters; and they may well be. But they are often symptomatic of a management which has never really considered environmental performance, or the benefits which can result from its improvement. As we have stressed in the previous chapter it is self-evident that if you conserve energy to reduce the generation of harmful combustion products you also reduce your fuel consumption, but all too often management has never made the effort to realize such benefits.

Another useful indicator is to look again at any comments or complaints your company may have received from the public—or from workers—about perceived environmental impacts. Are there a series of small incidents which have been dealt with as they occurred, but which might again be symptomatic of a common management weakness? Or is there something more significant which still requires effort to solve, but has been 'on the back-burner' for some time? In Chapter 7 we illustrate how complaints can be turned to advantage.

Even in the best run companies some examples like these will be found. They should provide the catalyst to convince senior management that a more thorough examination will uncover further, and possibly more significant, opportunities for improving environmental performance. This can often be achieved by an environmental audit.

The Environmental Audit

The United Nations Environment Programme has defined an Environmental Audit as a management tool comprising:

> . . . a systematic, documented, periodic and objective evaluation of how well
> environmental organization, management and equipment are performing with the
> aim of helping to safeguard the environment by facilitating management control of
> environmental practices and assessing compliance with company policies which
> would include meeting regulatory requirements.

You will see that such an environmental audit has much in common with a financial audit. Both require an audit trail, that is, a means of satisfying all parties that financial or environmental probity has been demonstrated. It is perhaps not surprising that most of our best known financial auditors have moved into the environmental auditing business as well!

While there is merit in an environmental audit being undertaken by a completely independent team, as formally it should, there are also advantages in involving your own staff, partly as a training exercise but also because in most technical businesses there will be much that the external auditor will not be familiar with and a long and expensive learning process can be avoided. A good, cost-effective compromise is for key members of the organization to undertake the audit in collaboration with one or two independent members added to the team from a reputable consultancy organization. It is likely then that subsequent 'periodic evaluations' mentioned in the UNEP definition can then be undertaken wholly in-house, with an external consultant providing 'verification' of the final audit report on the basis of a relatively small contract. An example of this approach is contained in the UK British Nuclear Fuels Plc Environmental Reports for 1992 and 1993. These contain a one-page verification statement from independent consultants which, while generally endorsing the document, identifies a few weaknesses in some of the reporting methods. The readers, who in this case include the public, will certainly look for the specific weaknesses to be remedied in subsequent reports! Examples of other reports with verification or review statements include those from the BP Company plc, The Body Shop International plc and National Power plc.

It would be inappropriate to set out any standard format for an audit. This must depend on the company and the nature of its business, and the format should be developed by the audit team. In principle it should address all inputs and outputs (including pollutants and wastes as key outputs) and assess the manner in which material flows within the plant influence the general environmental quality of the activities. Chapter 6 covers many of the factors which may be pertinent, but a general checklist can also be helpful, if only to set down reasons for concentrating attention on specific aspects. One such checklist is shown in Appendix 1, based on that included in the Open University course 'Enterprise and the Environment'. Notice how the supply chain is brought into this checklist with questions on the life cycle of a product or service.

Self-imposed Compliance Criteria and Legislation

Our definition of auditing also includes measuring compliance with company policies and legislation. This is clearly all important. No book can attempt to present a full picture of national, let alone international pollution legislation. In the UK we have over one hundred Acts of Parliament with some environmental content, and the European Union has many Directives which have to be satisfied as well. Furthermore, the legislative pattern is continually changing and it is imperative every company has the means of keeping up to date with compliance requirements.

Trade Associations play a key role in ensuring members are well briefed, and often set formal environmental performance requirements on their members as a condition of continuing membership. A good example is the Chemical Industries Association (CIA) 'Responsible Care' programme in the UK,[1] following a Canadian initiative from 1984. The cornerstone is an undertaking, signed by chief executives, to a set of guiding principles requiring their companies to make health, safety and environmental performance an integral part of their overall business policy. The undertaking also requires that all employees and company contractors are made aware of the commitment.

The guiding principles also require companies to:

- Conform to statutory regulations.
- Operate to the best practices of the industry.
- Assess the actual and potential . . . environmental impacts of their activities and products.
- Work closely with the authorities and the community in achieving the required levels of performance.
- Be open about activities and give relevant information to interested parties.

The Responsible Care programme was introduced by the CIA in 1989 and since 1992 the signatory commitment has been a condition of membership of the Association. It brings with it the added advantage that it has been designed to enable member companies to have their management systems certified to the International Standards Organization (ISO) series of quality standards ISO9000 mentioned in Chapter 2.

A further advantage of such a scheme is that by monitoring the performance of member companies the CIA gains access to much of the information it needs to undertake regular reviews across the industry as a whole. For instance, the CIA has collated the material and has published a report of UK Indicators of Performance from 1990 to 1992.[2] This includes capital and operating costs for environmental protection, discharges of noxious substances and disposal of special wastes and reductions in energy consumption, as well as trends in the number of complaints received over the years in question.

Apart from trade association documents there are many popular publications which are ideal for current awareness information; for example the *ENDS Reports*[3] provide a very effective service in the UK. Another source is the regular updates provided by major consultancy companies—the Environmental Digests of Lovell, White and Durrant[4] are examples while the PHAROS database from National Westminster Bank plc is a useful, interactive computer programme for analysing opportunities and obligations under the single European market and environmental legislation. There are also numerous professional bodies who are now in a position to give assistance with environmental matters. Appendix 3 lists a few in the UK, together with some international organizations and directories.

However, there are many features of national laws which are generally common, since international influences have played such a large part in defining environmental problems. The Environmental Protection Agency (EPA) in the USA took an early lead and many of the criteria now adopted stem directly from its initiatives. More recently the European Union has been very active and the requirements of its Directives are required to be incorporated into the national laws of Member States. West European countries outside the Union tend to have similar standards and East European countries are also moving towards following them. Other major industrial nations share experience through the Organization for Economic Co-operation and Cultural Development (OECD) and developing countries look to the United Nations for guidance. Nowadays developed and developing countries are often requiring the highest standards for new plants, particularly if they are operated by multinational companies who often work to the most stringent national standards at all of their international sites.

In general, regulation can be at a local or a national level. Often the less polluting processes, which are considered to have only 'local' effects on the environment, are controlled by local authorities with a limited geographical remit. In England such local authorities deal with solid wastes, noise, odour and the less polluting discharges to air. They also play a part with the National Rivers Authority (NRA) in regulating effluent discharges to watercourses. However, the more polluting processes and effluents containing prescribed noxious substances are regulated by a national body, Her Majesty's Inspectorate of Pollution (HMIP).

HMIP is responsible for implementing the principal regulatory duties under the system of Integrated Pollution Control (IPC). IPC applies to specified processes or prescribed pollutants (the latter are listed in Appendix 4) generated by:

- The fuel and power industries
- Metal production and processing
- Mineral industries
- The chemical industry
- Waste disposal and recycling
- Other specified industries (including paper and pulp manufacture)
- Di-isocyanate processes, processes involving uranium or thorium, coating processes, dyestuffs, printing ink manufacture
- The nuclear industry (not strictly IPC, but regulated by HMIP in a similar manner to IPC)

The processes which fall under IPC may only be operated following the issue of a formal authorization by HMIP. Failure to obtain such an authorization, or to satisfy the conditions within it, is a statutory offence punished by fines or imprisonment. Inspectors also have extensive powers, including the power to close forthwith plants which do not satisfy the conditions of an authorization and, in the view of the inspector, present an immediate environmental hazard.

The objectives of IPC are twofold:

1   To prevent the release of prescribed substances or, where that is not practicable, to reduce their release to a minimum and to render harmless any such substances which are so released.
2   To render harmless any other substances which might cause harm if released.

HMIP has a duty to ensure that authorized processes satisfy these objectives by:

- Ensuring that, in carrying on a prescribed process, the best available techniques not entailing excessive cost (BATNEEC) are used.
- Minimizing pollution to the environment as a whole, having regard to the best practicable environmental option (BPEO) if prescribed substances could be released to more than one medium or in more than one way.
- Ensuring compliance with any directions given by the State for the implementation of international obligations.
- Compliance with any limits or requirements and quality standards set by the Secretary of State for the Environment.
- Compliance with any plan made by the State for limiting particular types of pollution.

The concepts of BPEO and BATNEEC will be discussed in detail in Chapter 4. The other objectives enable the UK Government to meet international limits or quality standards, for instance on discharges of sulphur dioxide, nitrogen dioxide and CFCs which can have transfrontier consequences, and also to meet any national environmental quality standards (EQS) for the receiving media, which could require discharges lower than would result from strict application of BATNEEC and BPEO.

The European Union is following this IPC concept in its own legislation and Appendix 5 summarizes major principles of IPPC. It is reasonable to expect the integrated approach to spread among member states and elsewhere in the world. In the UK moves towards an Environmental Agency will certainly extend the concept, initially by bringing solid waste and all water regulation under the central agency, and doubtless later by assimilating many of the remaining waste regulation functions of local authorities. As concern with pollution grows, more centralization of control seems inevitable. An integrated system of pollution control has attractions to business through eliminating the need for multiple applications to different authorities for authorizations. It also facilitates discussion and consultation before permits are granted, assuming that such preliminary discussions are customary, as is the case in the Netherlands, for example.

External Quality Assurance Checks

The environmental audit has given you a snapshot of your current pollution performance, and contact with your regulators should have shown you what they will expect of you in the years to come. How do you set about achieving these targets?

The first step is to ensure that the appropriate management systems are in place. In the UK a very effective way to set up quality systems is to follow the principles set out by the UK British Standard Institution in a formal standard on Quality Systems, commonly known as BS5750.[5] This reflects other international schemes, such as those embodied in the International Standards Organization ISO9000 series mentioned earlier. BS5750 has its origins in general manufacturing industry, and it sets down a set of commonsense ideas aimed at ensuring that the customer will be satisfied with a product or service, while at the same time improving the supplier's efficiency. It provides interlocking checks and counterchecks, not only on the output, but equally on the initial planning and construction and implementation. The main sections of the standard are:

- Management responsibility
- Quality system
- Contract review
- Design control
- Purchasing
- Purchaser supplied products

- Product identification and traceability
- Process control
- Inspection and testing
- Inspection, measurement and test equipment
- Inspection and test status
- Control of non-conforming product
- Corrective action
- Handling, storage, packaging and delivery
- Quality records
- Internal quality audit
- Training
- Servicing
- Statistical techniques

While many of these sections have no direct bearing on environmental quality, they represent the type of management system for which any responsible company should strive. Indeed, accreditation to BS5750 is increasingly becoming a requirement for tendering for major work packages in the UK.

Of particular relevance to our interests we can translate quality concepts into environmental management concepts, and we can stress:

1 *Management responsibility.* Calling for the clear identification of responsibilities and for periodic reviews of the overall system.
2 *Contract review.* Bear in mind that an authorization or consent is a contract. This section ensures that each party is aware of what the authorization demands, it requires ambiguities to be clarified and the provision of adequate resources to fulfil the contract, often of crucial significance if major capital commitments are required to upgrade plant.
3 *Design control.* Applicable to new pollution control systems and monitoring. Waste minimization, BPEO aspects.
4 *Product identification and traceability.* Remember that wastes are 'products' even if unwanted ones.
5 *Handling, storage, packaging and delivery.* Equally appropriate to wastes. The Duty of Care in the UK places particular emphasis on these aspects for solid wastes, while the packaging laws developing throughout Europe are having a major impact.
6 *Quality records.* Perhaps the most important aspect, to ensure adequate control systems are in place, and can be shown to be in place.
7 *Internal quality audits.* Self-assessment by the team trained in the first environmental audit.
8 *Training.* Another important aspect. The features identified at the beginning of this chapter can only be dealt with on a day-to-day basis by good shop-floor practices and a work-force aware of the environment and what role they can play to protect it.

While the informal adoption of the principles embodied in BS5750 is laudable, the formal accreditation by an organization like the British Standards Institution should be the objective. This will entail inspection of the systems when in place and their regular review by the Standards Office. The kudos arising from accreditation should not be dismissed either since for 15 years it has been held in high esteem.

However, BS5750 was developed for general manufacturing industry, and although its scope has widened over the years it is not specifically aimed at environmental matters. This was recognized by the BSI and resulted in a standard on Environmental Management Systems, i.e. BS7750.[6] The sections of BS7750 are:

- Commitment
- Initial review
- Promulgating the environmental policy
- Organization and personnel
- Preparing a register of regulations
- Evaluation and register of effects
- Setting objectives and targets
- Development of management programmes
- Preparing a management manual
- Setting operational controls
- Records
- Audits
- Reviews
- Input to review of environmental policy

You will see that it follows fairly closely the structure of BS5750, but concentrates on environmental matters. In particular, an accredited company is required to have a clear environmental policy, full knowledge of the environmental effects of its activities, more extensive documentation setting up audit trails and formal audit and review procedures.

One key feature is the specification of a series of linked stages for the implementation of the environmental management scheme. The review feeds back into policy and starts another reappraisal of the cycle. The system is new and has yet to be proven, with the first registrations of organizations meeting the standard being awarded in 1994. However the system shows great promise, and companies should be aware of the methodology which underpins it.

Encouraging Environmental Awareness

Key features of any successful environmental improvement programme are management and worker commitment, already mentioned in the previous chapter. The first stage in obtaining the commitment should be through a formal environmental policy backed by the senior management and available to all staff. The policy need not, indeed should not, be long—one side of an A4 sheet is a good upper limit—and it should set out the company's objectives in clear, but not quantitative, terms. There should be provision for the policy to be updated from time to time as situations change, but probably not on a scheduled basis.

A good example of such a policy statement has been produced by the British Petroleum Company, plc. BP have worked to Health, Safety and Environmental policy statements for many years, but in 1991, with the onset of new legislation, the policy was revised to stress the importance of integrating the principles into every aspect of the group's business. The policy was widely distributed throughout the company and elsewhere as a booklet[7] which included a number of examples of how the policy was being implemented. The Managing Director signed the introduction and invited interested individuals and organizations to write to him with comments or suggestions.

The policy set out at that time is reproduced below:

BP strives to be an industry leader in health and safety practices and in environmental standards (HSE). We believe that good HSE performance is an integral part of efficient and profitable business management. We therefore intend to improve our HSE performance, and will be guided by the following principles:

Provide safe and healthy operations.

We will strive to create a working environment where accidents will not occur and in which employees, customers, contractors and the public will not be exposed to health hazards. Our employees and site contractors will be trained in workplace health and safety and will be encouraged to adopt a healthy lifestyle.

Produce and market products which can be used safely.

All products that BP makes for sale or use, and products rebranded by BP, will be evaluated to ensure that, despite inherent hazards, they can be stored, handled, transported and used safely. We will advise our customers on the safe use of our products, and on their disposal without adverse impact.

Progressive improvement in our environmental performance.

We will protect the environment by seeking to minimize the impact of our activities. We will strive for progressive improvement in the environmental performance of our facilities by reducing emissions, wastes and the use of energy. New facilities and plant will apply the best available pollution control techniques that are commercially viable.

Respect the interests of our neighbours and the world community.

We will communicate openly with those who live or work in the vicinity of our facilities to ensure their understanding of our operations, and our understanding of their concerns. We will also seek to participate actively with governments, other relevant bodies and the public in resolving HSE issues associated with our operations and products.

We will measure our HSE performance on a continuing basis against objectives established regularly for BP as a whole and for our individual businesses. We will have due regard to the concerns of our customers, employees, suppliers, local communities and the public in establishing our HSE standards and performance targets.

This policy applies to all BP group companies, and to all activities over which BP has control. In all other circumstances BP actively encourages the adoption of this policy.

This replaces the previous BP group HSE policy published in June 1982.

There are several points which are illustrated by the BP approach.

1 Safety, health and the environment are linked together. This makes sense since worker safety and environmental protection are usually closely related. While environmental protection includes all living species and the physical environment, it is generally accepted that if human health is protected at the individual level, then species of other living systems will also be protected. In general, the physical environment also responds to the same types of pressures as humans.
2 Hazards of storage, transport and handling are treated generally, and the policy applies equally to wastes, materials and products.
3 The environmental targets are paraphrases of the concepts described earlier under IPC, particularly waste minimization and BATNEEC.
4 Public concerns are addressed and dealt with.
5 Reference to targets leads naturally into the next phase of an environmental protection strategy—improvements.

We commend this type of approach to all organizations, particularly if coupled with regular staff newsletters highlighting progress and reminding readers of the policy. For example, BP supplements its policy statement with a number of supporting publications including *The Facts*, an annual update of how environmental performance is improving at all sites, and *New Horizons* which incudes world-wide summaries of environmental performance and what the company plans to do in the future. In Chapter 7 we deal with these aspects of communication in more detail and place them in the context of a corporate environmental management programme.

A survey of over 300 companies in the UK for the Institute of Directors[8] revealed that board agendas included environmental issues in 65 per cent of cases in 1992 compared with 53 per cent in 1991, and time for these issues is expected to grow. However, only 28 per cent of companies had an environmental policy and it was evident that many had still to introduce formal environmental programmes. Subsequent evidence suggested a rapid growth in the numbers of environmental managers as we have described previously. Examples of the organizational structures of several companies which have addressed these problems are available[9] and are supported by guidelines to stimulate organizations to develop their own programmes. Here we address some general principles.

Setting targets

After the environmental policy statement has been given effective publicity in your organization you can move on to setting specific targets for improvements. Many of these can be linked directly to financial savings, and there is no harm in making the link explicit. For instance, a convenient initial target for reducing energy use could be to limit expenditure on it to last year's cost, or even to look for, say, a 5 per cent saving.

Waste Minimization, Recycling and 'Clean' Technology

Waste minimization, recycling and the adoption of 'clean' technology are means whereby direct returns through reductions of raw material purchases can be realized. Recently the UK Centre for Exploitation of Science and Technology (CEST) set up a co-operative waste minimization project[10] in the north of England. Eleven companies were involved and over 200 potential savings valued at about £2m per annum were identified initially (Table 3.1). Subsequently the number of waste minimization measures grew to over 520, with only 2 per cent being impracticable. Since the project cost about £400 000 the payback period is remarkably short. This study, known as the Aire and Calder Project, is described in more detail in Chapter 6. Further, similar studies are now under way.

A number of other examples of similar savings have been presented by the UK Department of Trade and Industry in two free publications: *Cutting Your Losses* and *Cutting Your Losses 2*.[11] The examples include savings from a waste audit, materials substitution, waste and effluent reduction, reuse of process water or solvent, better control monitoring, recycling and finding markets for by-products which would otherwise be treated as wastes. The companies involved range from the largest (Bayer, Pilkington, Royal Ordnance, ICI) to

Table 3.1   Financial benefits from waste minimization opportunities in Aire and Calder Project (CEST)

Company	Annual saving (£)
British Rail	290 000
Coca-Cola	1 600 000
Croda Colours	25–30 000
Crystal Drinks	30 000
Du Pont Howson	63 000
Rhone-Poulenc	25 000
Warwick International	85 000

small companies with as few as 19 employees. Payback periods are often less than a year and rarely more than three years, and it is often possible to get limited financial support from national trade departments or the EU for novel schemes which could have a more general application. There can be few companies incapable of making some environmental and financial savings in this way.

Packaging

Packaging materials also offer considerable opportunities for material and waste economies. In developed countries discarded packaging now represents as much as 40 per cent of municipal waste. The Digital Equipment Corporation (DEC) in the USA have estimated that it used to require 27 000 tonnes of packaging materials annually, costing about $54m. There is clearly great incentive to reduce this quantity for economic as well as environmental reasons, and the DEC has now reduced packaging volumes by up to 90 per cent on a wide range of products.

In some countries the use of packaging is now being restricted by legislative means. In Germany the law requires that by mid-1995 80 per cent of packaging materials must be reused and recycled. This law affects not only German companies, but also those exporting into Germany, and is becoming a significant factor for a number of them. In Denmark, where there are already controls on the use of aluminium cans and taxes on packaging, there are plans to completely ban the use of polyvinyl chloride containers and packs. Italy is introducing specific taxes and Dutch industry has to reduce packaging materials by 10 per cent by the year 2000. While packaging is clearly necessary to protect and enhance the marketability of products there is much that can be done to reduce quantities, such as:

- Redesigning the packaging structure to eliminate unnecessary layers, as DEC did in computer packaging.
- Modifying production and/or product design of existing packaging to reduce weight, for example by a pharmaceutical firm now using plastic containers in place of glass.
- Using more environmentally acceptable materials, preferably those which are biodegradable, for example fast food chains phasing out the use of polystyrene foam containers for beverages and hamburgers, and replacing them with paper based products.
- Compacting packaging materials, such as expanded polystyrene, to facilitate its transport and recycling.
- Recycling packaging films, such as polyethylene around bulk deliveries, for use in other products such as refuse sacks.

Recycling

In New York it now costs over $100 per tonne to landfill domestic refuse. As landfill protection standards rise and landfill sites become more scarce these costs will be reflected in many other developed countries and the pressure for recycling will grow as much for economic as for environmental reasons. There is still much which can be done as Table 3.2 illustrates.[12]

Europe is proposing to tackle the problem by requiring at least 50 per cent of all packaging materials to be recycled by 2005. Similar laws are being introduced, or exist, in the majority of developed countries. Cars represent a special case for recycling and there is now pressure from governments in Europe and the USA to make the car manufacturer responsible for the cradle to grave life of the vehicles produced. This is leading to better segregation of plastics in components, the phasing out of environmentally unfriendly metals, like lead and chromium, together with the adoption of manufacturing techniques which improve opportunities for material segregation when the vehicle is scrapped. Volkswagen, BMW and Opel have already introduced policies of taking back vehicles free for recycling. This trend will grow and spread from the motor industry into other areas of manufacturing. IBM in the UK, for instance, now accepts scrap computers and recycles most of the materials. Similarly other electronics industries are moving from breaking up items for disposal in landfill, to exploiting recovery of components after disassembly, sometimes by external organizations.

Table 3.2   Proportion of waste recycled, 1991. (Source: *The Economist*, 13 April 1991)

Product	Location	Annual kg/person	Waste recycled (%)
Paper	Western Europe	170–180	40–45
	Japan	170	50
	USA	270	25
Aluminium	Western Europe	18–20	30
	Japan	22	40
	USA	10	32
Glass	Western Europe	25	30
	Japan	7	55
	USA	50	12
Plastic	Western Europe	17	5
	Japan	25	0
	USA	55	1

Best available techniques

Perhaps the most important aspect of improving performance is the adoption of best available techniques for reducing the environmental impact of discharges and wastes. This is certainly the aspect that most legislation concentrates upon, and as a result pressure will arise from regulators as much as, and probably more than, from in-house or public expressions of environmental concerns. A useful senior management approach, adopted by ICI as an example, is to link the policy statement with a general commitment to reduce wastes to, say, half in the next decade. Again, such statements do much to develop a corporate dedication to the objective, and can serve a useful function in loosening purse strings if finance becomes hard to find. Another approach by multinationals is to make a commitment that all plants in all countries will operate to the most stringent environmental standards anywhere in the world. Such statements should ensure that plant operating in countries with less environmentally advanced legislation do not become the company's 'dustbin', taking all the dirty processes which are not acceptable elsewhere.

Notwithstanding such commitments, it is always worth carrying out a thorough survey of new developments in the environmental protection field before introducing expensive new plant. It is not the purpose of this book to rank pollution abatement equipment, which is developing very rapidly this decade with the advent of more sensitive systems and computer control technologies. There are growing databases of such equipment, which are regularly updated by independent bodies. For example, the US Environmental Protection Agency has developed VISITT (Vendor Information System for Innovative Treatment Technologies).[13] This provides current information on a wide range of innovative land remediation technologies, based on a freely available computer disc access system. It is regularly updated, and is invaluable to those involved in the clean-up of contaminated sites. An example of a print-out is included in Chapter 6 where the system is described in more detail.

National agencies also provide their own updates of available techniques and the level of pollution abatement they are capable of achieving. In the UK, examples include a series of over 100 guidance notes prepared by HMIP dealing with the processes prescribed under IPC,[14] and another set from the Secretary of State for the Environment[15] dealing with those processes with a potential to cause air pollution which are regulated by local authorities. Similar guidance relating to water pollution is being provided by the NRA.[16]

Apart from published information of this type much is to be gained from informal discussions with regulators. They will normally be up to date on technological developments, and will have discussed them with organizations similar to your own. They will know of the problems and can often guide you in an informal way to solving them. However, a possible problem with this approach is that the regulators may look for a gold-plated solution to a problem, without too much regard to what your company regards as excessive cost. In such a case you may not have the technical expertise to refute the regulator's proposal, and there could be merit in commissioning an expert consultant to prepare and present your case for somewhat less stringent standards. Your trade association may be able to help directly, or suggest appropriate consultants to you.

While it will be in the interests of the environmentally conscious company to set targets for reducing pollution, these may well be imposed anyway by regulators. For instance, IPC requires inspectors who authorize the continuing operation of existing plant, which may not meet present day standards, to set down in the authorization a timetable with clear milestones to upgrade the plant. It is essential in such circumstances to ensure that all options are explored in developing a cost-effective timetable and plan, and again the assistance of an independent consultant could well be helpful.

Options for Off-site Disposal

It is no longer enough to arrange for a contractor to remove your bulk waste, and when the waste has gone away to conclude that you are absolved from the consequences of any problems it may later pose. Many countries now have a continuing absolute liability on waste producers, effectively for all time, while in others there may be a temporal or geographical cut-off, for instance, at the disposal step. Waste producers must, therefore, have an understanding of the factors which determine acceptably safe disposal and be able to select the most appropriate for each waste stream.

The first requirement is to identify all waste streams and to appreciate the chemical and physical composition of your wastes. The waste audit will have gone a long way to meeting this objective, but you will probably need more specific information before proceeding to commit waste to a particular disposal route. Producers should be aware of the presence of particular environmentally sensitive contaminants, i.e. chlorinated materials, asbestos, heavy metals, clinical waste, which may have a profound effect on the disposal route selected and the resulting disposal costs. Clinical waste management forms the basis for our fifth case history (Chapter 8, Section 5), but the general concepts apply to any really hazardous solid waste. Our case history shows that when it is possible to segregate such materials this should be done. Dilute and disperse in a waste stream is no longer an environmentally acceptable option.

Attention must also be paid to the physical nature of the waste. Sludges can be particularly difficult, and some disposal routes are inappropriate for solid or liquid wastes. For example, incineration is unlikely to lessen the environmental impact of heavy metals, and flammable solvents or volatile organic compounds should not be disposed of in landfills. Where mixing of wastes occurs, during treatment, transport or disposal, the reactivity and compatibility of the mixture must be considered to eliminate any risk of explosion, fire or the release of noxious vapours.

The location of disposal facilities could affect the viability of certain options. Factors to be borne in mind include the ease with which the material can be transported, the location of bottlenecks and access arrangements at the receiving site. In most countries incinerators capable of dealing with hazardous wastes are few and far between, which may well encourage recycling or chemical treatment if landfill is inappropriate, as it probably will be. Indeed, many smaller countries have no suitable incinerators, and transfrontier shipments of hazardous wastes are now almost impossible.

Even when a suitable means has been identified, your responsibility should not end, and probably does not. Certainly the Duty of Care part of the UK Environmental Protection Act 1990 requires more, as we describe in Chapter 5 and in Appendix 2. For the most hazardous wastes it is prudent to visit the site to satisfy yourself about its management and record keeping; one company, on checking a waste disposal contractor's records, found that a consignment had apparently been disposed of before it had even left the producer's site! Such checks can require specialized skills, and some consulting companies now offer a service on a co-operative basis to regularly review disposal facilities on behalf of clients. Normally such checks should ensure that there is an effective audit trail, supported by records, from producer to final disposal, and probably involving directly tracking at least one consignment along that trail.

New Plant

So far we have assumed that you are seeking to improve the environmental performance of existing plant. Somewhat different criteria have to be applied to the planning, construction and operation of new plant. It is essential that management are aware that environmental issues will play a large part in getting local and national approval of any major development, and these should be considered from the start. Just as traditionally management has justified new plant on financial grounds, in future, environmental issues will require similar attention. Can the new plant meet standards specified as Best Available Pollution Abatement Techniques? The 'not entailing excessive cost' reservation has no place for new plant!

The initial planning consent will possibly require a formal Environmental Impact Assessment (EIA), but even if it does not, then it is prudent to have made one and record it as part of the justification for the plant. In any case a small study will be needed to establish if there are any ecologically sensitive areas which could be affected as a precursor to a full EIA. Poorly planned developments can result in unnecessary costs being incurred in revising planning applications. Bear in mind that in some circumstances even BAT may be insufficient to satisfy an inspector if he has to meet international quality standards for a particular component and the receiving medium is already loaded close to the limit.

A case in point occurred when an EC Directive set limits on the concentration of pentachlorophenol (PCP) in inland waters. In some parts of the UK imported cloth for making up into garments was found to contain considerable quantities of PCP which was used as an insect repellant. In working with the cloth the PCP was washed out and was discharged with laundry washing to local watercourses. Although the companies concerned were unaware of the presence of PCP the Directive limits were approached so closely that no new plant handling the cloth could discharge into the watercourses. The only option available was to collect all washings and transport them elsewhere by tanker for chemical treatment. In future such situations are likely to increase in number.

Do not assume that because a plant is new there will be no requirement to improve the quality of pollution abatement equipment. Most legislation makes provision for regular reviews of the quality of the technology to ensure that it remains 'best'. The Environmental Protection Act requires such reviews at least every four years, and EU proposals require similar reviews. While pollution abatement plant resulting from major capital expenditure must clearly be given the necessary opportunity to operate throughout its design life, the reviews will undoubtedly become an opportunity for fine tuning systems and thereby reducing the overall pollution potential of the plant. It is worth looking at what might be required in a few years' time and ensuring that designs have sufficient redundancy and flexibility to satisfy what may be demanded at that time.

Contaminated Land

The legacy of past environmental mismanagement has resulted in an estimated 50 000–100 000 contaminated sites in the UK with a total area of 100 000 hectares. Germany is reported to have 130 000 contaminated sites and the Netherlands 100 000. As much as 10 per cent of the land used by industry may be regarded as contaminated. This may be by oil from parking areas, but also from major industrial activities involving the most noxious substances like polychlorinated biphenyls and asbestos. Such contamination may well limit the value of a property or piece of land, changing an asset into a liability.

Banks and many companies in the property business, for instance GE Capital who deal with property on an international basis, are now requiring environmental assessments of any site before acquisition, to satisfy themselves about potential risks and liabilities, and possible costs of clean-up. It is something every industrialist must bear in mind whether the proposal is to acquire property or sell it. The information can be used by the parties to determine and negotiate the conditions of the transaction and may lead to purchase money hold backs or cost sharing arrangements for clean-up, or warranties to cover possible remediation of the consequences of historical practices.

Such assessments can usually be phased to reduce cost and increase value. The first phase is a preliminary environmental site assessment, commonly called a PESA. This is a non-intrusive study of the site and the surrounding properties, together with a review of historical records and local knowledge. If necessary this can be followed by a more detailed intrusive study to pinpoint and quantify contamination, to be followed by the final remedial phase.

In some circumstances where there is obvious contamination the first phase may appear unnecessary, but can still be cost-effective in bringing together all relevant information before spade is put to soil. Information could also be obtained on the following aspects of a site:

- The degree of soil and groundwater contamination arising from activities on or off the site over historic time.
- Followed by intrusive investigations by the installation of trial pits or bore-holes, and the sampling and chemical analysis of soil and/or groundwater.
- The degree of building contamination. This may come, for example, in the form of friable asbestos in deteriorated building materials such as fire proofing or building insulation. There may be indoor air pollution problems associated with hazardous dusts, particulates, radon or carbon monoxide. Legionnaires' disease may also be a problem in buildings with old air conditioning plant.
- The compliance of the manufacturing facility. Compliance audits can cover a wide range of issues such as occupational health, authorization of scheduled processes, discharge consents or Duty of Care with waste disposal.

Conclusion

The term 'environmental assurance' has been used as a development from the concepts of quality assurance and of environmental audits.[17] As such it builds on the standard procedures for analysing and improving the environmental performance of an organization.

Environmental assurance is an extended audit programme including the technology for production, the management system and the external relationship with government and the community. Integrating these components into a management system not only minimizes the environmental impact of operations, but also enhances company profit, growth and survival. Incorporating these concepts into your organization will also facilitate meeting your legal obligations.

Practical Points for Action

- Start with a simple and superficial audit.
- Always try to audit in-house to develop knowledge which remains within the organization, with external quality assurance checks.
- Develop and promulgate an environmental policy.
- Publish an environmental statement.
- Set clear and meaningful targets for improvements, and ensure all are aware of progress towards their achievement.
- Consult your trade association to avoid having to rediscover known truths.
- Check to see if a rigorous integrated pollution abatement approach can be justified by your organization's activities.
- Ensure staff are aware of environmental issues by effective training and information supply.
- Make sure you are exercising 'Duty of Care'.

References

1   Chemical Industries Association, *Responsible Care*, CIA, Kings Buildings, Smith Square, London, SW11P 3PJ, 1992.

2   Chemical Industries Association, *UK Indicators of Performance*, CIA, Kings Buildings, Smith Square, London, SW1P 3PJ, 1993.

3   *ENDS Reports*, Environmental Data Services Ltd, Finsbury Business Centre, 40 Bowling Green Lane, London, EC1R 0NE.

4   Lovell, White and Durrant, 65 Holborn Viaduct, London, EC1A 2DY and in New York, Paris, Brussels, Prague, Hong Kong, Beijing and Tokyo.

5   BSI, *Quality Systems*, BS5750, British Standards Institution, Linford Wood, Milton Keynes, MK14 6LE.

6   BSI, *Environmental Management Systems*, BS7750, British Standards Institution, Linford Wood, Milton Keynes, MK14 6LE, 1993.

7   BPC, *New Horizons 1991*, British Petroleum Company, plc, Brittanic House, 1 Finsbury Circus, London, EC2M 7BA.

8   Institute of Directors, *IoD Members Opinion Survey: Environment*, Director Publications, London, 1993.

9   'Companies' Organisation and Public Communication on Environmental Issues', UNEP/IEO, Paris, 1992.

10   CEST, *Aire & Calder Project*, March Consultants, Salford Keys, Manchester, M5 2XW, 1993.

11   DTI, *Cutting Your Losses* and *Cutting Your Losses 2*, The Department of Trade & Industry Enterprise Initiative, Bridge Place, 88/89 Eccleston Square, London, SW11V 1PT.

12   *The Economist*, 13 April 1991.

13   VISITT, US Environmental Protection Agency/NCEPI, PO Box 42419, Cincinnati, Ohio OH45242-0419. 3rd Revision, 1994.

14 Chief Inspector's Guidance to Inspectors, Environmental Protection Act 1990; HMSO, PO Box 276, London, SW8 5DT for a complete list of notes.

15 Environmental Protection Act 1990, Secretary of State's Guidance on Processes Prescribed for Air Pollution Control by Local Authorities, HMSO, PO Box 276, London, SW8 5DT for a complete list.

16 National Rivers Authority, Rivers House, Waterside Drive, Aztec West, Bristol, BS12 4UD.

17 J. A. Huggard, C. P. George, and A. M. Warris, *Environmental Pollution 1, ICEP-1, Proceedings*, vol. 1, Inderscience, Geneva, 1991.

4

Assessment

In the previous chapter we have considered how to measure and improve a company's environmental performance. We have defined performance in simple terms: environmental awareness in purchasing raw materials, staff training, reduction in waste, minimization of discharges. However, to quantify these improvements in terms relevant to environmental protection can be extremely difficult and rarely will it be possible to be precise. HMIP have proposed a general environmental procedure which, if it can be applied, will lead to the determination of the best practicable environmental option (BPEO) for the process, taking account of the best available techniques not entailing excessive cost (BATNEEC). The procedure is set out in Table 4.1. As some of the terms may be new to the reader these are defined in the notes below the table.

Best Available Techniques and the Best Practicable Environmental Option

As we have stated in earlier chapters, BAT and its derivative BATNEEC, or formulations which are equivalent in meaning, are gaining increasing favour in international legislation and agreements. However, there remains considerable confusion about the meaning of the terms and their application. The UK has set down working definitions[1] on which this and subsequent sections are based.

'Best' could mean that only one of the great variety of technical options available for dealing with a particular pollutant is acceptable. However, if best is taken as providing the best pollution control solution by preventing, minimizing or rendering harmless the emissions concerned, then there may well be more than one set of techniques which will be equally effective. As a consequence by using achievable emission levels as the regulatory tool rather than trying to define a specific technique there may well be more than one 'best' solution, and industry will not be discouraged from seeking innovative solutions to problems.

Table 4.1 The Assessment Procedure used by HMIP in the UK

Procedure	Comments
Stage 1: Select practicable process options	*Stage 1* A range of process or abatement techniques should be selected by the operator which are consistent with or better than the standards set by the regulators. In the case of new plant a wider range of options should be considered compared with existing plant where the practicable options may be constrained by plant conditions.
Stage 2: Environmental assessment Assessment of harm	*Stage 2*
Step 1: Identify pollutants released	Step 1: For each process and abatement option identify the unavoidable releases of prescribed and other substances.
Step 2: Determine compliance with environmental quality standards and regulatory assessment limits (RALs)*	Step 2: Releases which lead to a breach of an environmental quality standard (specific or inferred) should not be authorized.
Step 3: Identify significant releases	Step 3: A release can be considered significant if the predicted environmental concentration (PEC)‡ is greater than the action level§ *and* the plant contribution is > 1% of the relevant EQS or RAL.
Step 4: Assess short-term effects of significant releases	Step 4: Assess short-term effects of releases for both existing and new plant. If the short-term PEC + peak ambient concentration is greater than the short-term guideline for the substance then further evaluation is needed. Amend process options considered if necessary.
Assessment of best environmental option	
Step 5: Calculate BPEO Index†	Step 5:Normalize significant releases as a proportion of the EQS or RAL. For each process option sum Tolerability Quotients across all significant substances and media.
Step 6: Rank process options according to BPEO Index	Step 6: Rank the process options according to the BPEO Index. The BEO can be considered to be the option for which the BPEO Index value is the lowest so long as the short term consequences of the releases are tolerable.
Stage 3:Determination of site-specific BPEO/BATNEEC	*Stage 3*
Step 7: Select option as site-specific BATNEEC. Is this the best environmental option?	Step 7: From the range of options considered the operator should select the preferred technique. If this represents the BEO then no further analysis is required.
Step 8: Assess case for departure from best environmental option	Step 8: If the BEO is not selected then the chosen option should be justified on grounds of excessive costs or (more rarely) for environmental considerations.
Step 9: Determine site-specific BPEO/BATNEEC	Step 9: Confirm selection of process option as site-specific BATNEEC.

* Regulatory Assessment Limit: The long-term average concentration of a substance which for the purpose of assessing the BPEO the Regulatory Body regards as the maximum value permissible in the environmental medium concerned at that location.
† BPEO Index: The ranking of a series of environmental options and the weightings afforded to them.
‡ Predicted environmental concentration: The total predicted concentration of a substance expected at a given location.
§ Action level: The concentration of a substance at a location, below which with present knowledge, the environmental consequences of a release can be considered negligible.

'Available' could refer to any process which has been reported in the scientific literature, or demonstrated at a bench scale in a research laboratory. You can see many such techniques listed in the VISITT database described previously. Alternatively, a company may have a very effective proprietary process which has been patented and which the company will not licence to its competitors. In practice, 'available' should be taken to mean procurable by the operator of the process in question. It should be a technique which has been developed or proven at a scale which allows the implementation in the relevant industrial context with the necessary commercial confidence of its success. It does not imply that sources outside the country concerned are 'unavailable'. Nor does it imply a competitive supply market. If there is a monopoly supplier the technique is available only so long as the operator can procure it.

'Techniques' embraces both the process and how the process is operated. It should be taken to mean the concept and design of the process, the components of which it is made up and the manner in which they are connected together to make a whole. It also includes matters such as numbers and qualifications of staff, working methods, training and supervision and also the design, construction, layout and maintenance of buildings.

The concept NEEC (not entailing excessive costs) should be considered in two contexts, depending on whether it is applied to new processes (including those undergoing substantial variation, such that they can be regarded as 'new') or existing processes. For new processes the presumption should be that BAT be required. There can be little justification, if any, for designing and operating new plant to pollution control standards other than the best which current techniques can deliver. Existing processes cannot always be expected to meet such stringent standards overnight, but timescales should be established for upgrading the plant to current standards for new plant, or if that is not possible, to have a programme leading to eventual decommissioning and replacement. In setting timescales attention will need to be given to the particular plant's technical characteristics, to its rate of utilization and length of remaining life and the nature and volume of polluting emissions from it.

For any given process there may be a range of 'techniques' which could be used to reduce any given pollutant, all of which could lead to a similar outcome in terms of environmental pollution abatement. Furthermore, there could be a number of environmentally sensitive products, each of which could require a different scenario of techniques. An example could be the pollution which could arise from a coal-fired combustion process. In terms of airborne discharges there is a range of desulphurization processes which could reduce sulphur dioxide emissions. Another set of actions could be put in place to reduce emissions of nitrogen oxides; still others could reduce dust and grit emissions. Each pollutant would then have its own set of BAT (or BATNEEC) requirements for its amelioration; this would also apply to the control of discharges to water and the management of the various solid wastes, including ash.

Our next task is then to establish which sets of Best Available Techniques can then be applied together in an integrated way to minimize the total (integrated) environmental detriment. This will then be the Best Practicable Environmental Option (BPEO).

The BPEO has been defined by the UK Royal Commission on Environmental Pollution as:

> The outcome of a systematic consultative and decision-making procedure which emphasizes the protection of the environment across land, air and water. The BPEO procedure establishes, for a given set of objectives, the option that provides the most benefit, or least damage, to the environment as a whole, at acceptable cost, in the long term as well as the short term.

The process of selecting the BPEO is broken down into the following stages:

- Define objective
- Generate options
- Evaluate options
- Summarize and present evaluation
- Select preferred option
- Review preferred option
- Implement and monitor

The objective will normally be to minimize the overall environmental impact of a process when it is impractical to eliminate all pollutants from liquid or gaseous discharges, or from solid waste. It may be appropriate to consider each substance alone or with other components in the same or related waste streams. It will be necessary to define environmental impact in such a way that comparisons can be made between discharges to air or water or disposal in solid waste, by incineration, landfill or chemical treatment. Similarly, some means of comparing risks to man, fauna, flora and the physical environment will be required. Finally, the operator needs to be able to evaluate risks to local and global populations in the short and long term, and compare them.

The only industry to tackle these problems in a systematic way has been the nuclear industry. Radioactivity is easy to measure, there are a limited number of sources of it, and there is little historical 'contamination'. There are few chemical species involved and they tend to be specific to the nuclear industry.

In contrast, there is a relatively high background of chemical pollution, from natural sources (mineral ores, natural forest fires, photochemical reactions) as well as from human activities. There are many thousand chemical species involved and it is often impossible to find the specific source of any given pollution observation, particularly if it is at a low level. Many chemical species are very difficult to measure at low concentrations (e.g. dioxins, PCBs) and sometimes weeks may be required to get an accurate laboratory result, by which time the pollution concerned may have dispersed. Nevertheless, the approaches adopted by the nuclear industry are useful in defining a methodology for any BPEO study.

The first question to resolve is what targets to consider and how to compare them. Generally humans provide the key target to be protected, and the nuclear industry has assumed that any system protecting us at the individual level will protect other biological systems at the species level. In the chemical field there are obvious exceptions and defoliation due to acid rain and the death of birds due to pesticides are clear examples. Consideration must be given to such possibilities in setting objectives.

Having defined targets it is essential to have a measure of how pollutants damage the target, and if chemical speciation may influence the level of harm. Barium sulphate is almost insoluble and relatively harmless to humans. Barium chloride, on the other hand, is soluble in stomach acids and is highly toxic. The BPEO for a barium salt would therefore favour the sulphate salt rather than the chloride. An appropriate measure of harm from all possible chemical forms of potential pollutants has to be found.

The next step is to measure exposure of, and if possible uptake by, target groups. Uptake depends on dispersion paths and, while it may be possible to determine them by survey and chemical analysis for existing plant, there could well be problems due to background pollution from other sources, and temporal difficulties. It is always desirable to back up such measurements with mathematical models, which should, in principle, eliminate most of the unwanted signals. Such methods are inevitable for new plant when only predictive calculations are possible. Suitable computer programmes have been developed by a number of organizations, including government departments and professional consultants who should be able to provide assistance if needed.

With a knowledge of source concentrations and having determined pathways it should be possible to estimate received exposures. The nuclear industry selects two groups of targets: a critical group of those subject to the highest exposures and the population as a whole (township, country or the world) who receive a 'collective dose' expressed as the integrated exposure of the whole population group which can be summed over many generations. The critical group is obviously potentially at immediate risk and exposures must be kept as low as is practicable, and certainly below regulatory control standards. The public as a whole are exposed not just to substances from the operation of the plant in question, but also to similar discharges from other plant, and possibly quite different pollutants which may exercise a synergistic effect. Sometimes, national and international bodies will have set environmental quality standards for the receiving medium (in effect, the collective exposure), which should protect the public from long-term risks from low levels of the pollutants concerned. When this is not so the regulator has to set appropriate regulatory assessment levels which will serve a similar purpose. However, there remains a responsibility for the plant operator to minimize such effects in the choice of BPEO.

Comparison of immediate or short-term effects with long-term effects over many generations also poses problems. We need to compare a discharge to the sea which is rapidly dispersed in the deep oceans (but may expose those on the beach to a small risk for a few hours) with disposal to landfill, when pollutants may not return to the biosphere for centuries, but by which time a large conurbation drinking well-water may have been established just where the pollutant concentrates. Clearly risk analysis has to be used in dealing with uncertain scenarios such as these, and some discounting factor will normally be applied to the probabilistic long-term risks. There is, at present, no international agreement on what these factors should be.

Generating options is the next formal step in approaching the BPEO. This requires a knowledge of the options which are available and which will satisfy BAT requirements. There may be a number. Their evaluation requires the knowledge of pathways, targets and exposure patterns outlined above. In presenting the results care must be taken to ensure that bias has not entered the analysis due to lack of data about some of the pathways or options. If it has, the extent of the bias should be specified. Selection of the final BPEO is a matter for regulators, the operators and the managers to agree in concert, recognizing that it must stand the test of scrutiny in public records.

Table 4.1 shows how HMIP plans to use the concept of BATNEEC in its legislative role. It will primarily be seen as the means whereby an operator makes a case that the best environmental option (BEO) is inappropriate because of site-specific aspects of the process under consideration, and if this is duly accepted by the regulator then that technique is BATNEEC.

Example of a BPEO/BATNEEC Assessment for a Coal-fired Power Station

In the UK Her Majesty's Inspectorate of Pollution (HMIP) has applied the methodology to a generic 2000 MWe coal-fired power station consisting of four 500 MW generators.[2] For simplicity they have limited their detailed assessment of two potential pollutants, sulphur dioxide and nitrogen oxides, although other substances are considered more superficially. The methodology can, however, be applied to more complex situations.

Power station description

Before combustion, coal is ground to a fine powder in pulverising mills then mixed with hot air and blown into boilers. Waste gases from the boiler are passed through electrostatic precipitators to achieve greater than 90 per cent dust removal before discharge through a 200 m multi-flue stack.

Cooling water is abstracted from the nearby river. After use it is circulated through cooling towers before being returned to the condenser inlet for reuse. A proportion of the water is purged to the river and further water is abstracted to make up for abstraction losses. Liquid effluents generated on site include boiler blowdown, site drainage, sluice water from the ash pit and treated sewage effluent. These are passed through an oil interceptor to the ash settlement lagoons before discharge to the river. Pulverized fuel ash is pumped to settling lagoons from where the supernatant liquors are discharged to a second local water course. Furnace bottom ash is sluiced to the ash pit from which it is later removed, dried and transported off-site for final disposal or reuse as a construction material. The site is located alongside a major river. The surrounding area is principally mixed arable and grassland with a number of small rural communities.

Selection of practicable process options

The objective is that this existing plant should meet new performance standards by 2001. Some of the requirements could already be met with the current technology, for instance releases of particulates to air and mercury and cadmium to water. Others, such as reduction in sulphur dioxide and oxides of nitrogen, could not be achieved. A range of process and abatement technologies which were consistent with achieving them were then selected for evaluation. They were limestone/gypsum flue gas desulphurization (LG), spray dry flue gas desulphurization (SD), low-NOx burners (LNB), selective non-catalytic reduction (SNCR) and selective catalytic reduction (SCR). When the two sulphur abatement techniques are combined with the three nitrogen abatement techniques six overall process options are available.

Identification of Pollutants Released

The substances released are summarized in Table 4.2 for the base case operation.

Table 4.2 Substances released

Air	Water	Land
Sulphur dioxide	Suspended solids	Sulphur dioxide*
Oxides of nitrogen	Chloride	Oxides of nitrogen*
Particulates	Chlorine (biocide)	Heavy metals*
Hydrogen chloride	Heavy metals	Furnace bottom ash/PFA†
Heavy metals	Heat	FGD residues†

* Substances released to air followed by deposition to land.
† Substances disposed to landfill.

Assessment of compliance with environmental quality standards or regulatory assessment limits

For the base case there are no releases to air which lead to ambient concentrations greater than the EQS (Assessment of Compliance with Environmental Quality Standards) or RAL (the Regulatory Assessment Limit is set by the regulatory body in the absence of a formal EQS). Using any of the process options, concentrations remain below the acceptable levels. In the case of discharges to water the ambient concentrations of suspended solids are above the EQS value for both the main river and that receiving the supernatant from the PFA lagoons. Process options involving limestone/gypsum FGD are likely to release additional suspended solids to water and therefore these options are removed from further consideration.

Releases of heavy metals to air and their subsequent deposition to land does not lead to a breach of the deposition RALs for heavy metals. However, the deposition of nitrogen and sulphur compounds add significantly to the load on the area, which is sensitive to acidification. Action needs to be taken to reduce levels significantly.

Identification of significant releases

Table 4.2 shows that in total a wide variety of substances is released from the station, and there are other factors of concern such as Biological Oxygen Demand and suspended solids. It would be impracticable to make a complete environmental audit of each, and it is essential that the environmentally significant materials are targeted. The release of a substance is regarded as significant if the Predicted Environmental Concentration (PEC) is greater than the Action Level and the plant contribution is greater than 1 per cent of the Regulatory Assessment Level (see Table 4.1 footnotes for detailed definitions of terms). Table 4.3 identifies the significant releases based on these criteria.

Table 4.3 Environmentally significant releases

Air	Water	Land (via deposition)
Nitrogen dioxide	Suspended solids	Cadmium
Sulphur dioxide	Biochemical oxygen demand	Nickel
Hydrogen chloride	Cadmium	Sulphur
	Copper	Nitrogen

Assessment of Short-term Effects of Releases

In assessing the BPEO it is crucial to assess the short-term effects of releases. Since peak ambient and plant contributions may be separated temporally and spatially a detailed assessment required substantial effort and input of detailed data, as has been shown earlier. Sophisticated modelling may help if sufficiently reliable models are available. After the best analysis possible with the data available it was concluded that releases from any of the process options would not lead to adverse short-term effects for any of the environmentally significant pollutants.

The BPEO Index

The BPEO Index provides a semi-quantitative measure of the overall environmental consequences of each process option across all media, based on annual average data. For a particular process option the index is calculated as follows. A tolerability quotient (TQ) is derived for each substance and for each medium as the quotient of the predicted environmental concentration and the appropriate EQS or RAL. The TQ for release of all substances to a given medium are then summed to give a medium TQ, and these in turn are summed for all media to produce the BPEO Index.

In this way the Index is calculated for the range of process and abatement techniques under consideration, and the Best Environmental Option (BEO) will be represented by the system with the lowest index value.

Ranking process options according to the Index

A BPEO Index value was calculated for the base case operation of each of the three remaining process options. They are shown in rank order in Table 4.4.

Table 4.4   BPEO Indexes for selected options

Process/abatement option	BPEO Index
Base case operation	10.46
Spray dry FGD + low NOx burners	10.21
Spray dry FGD + SNCR	10.20
Spray dry FGD + SCR	10.19

The table also shows that the options selected lead to a significant reduction in the index when compared with the base case. Of the three options evaluated spray dry FGD with Selective Catalytic Reduction (SCR) produces the lowest index and can be considered the BEO.

Determination of site specific BPEO/BATNEEC

If the operator had selected the BEO for implementation then no further analysis would have been needed. However, in this case study the operator is

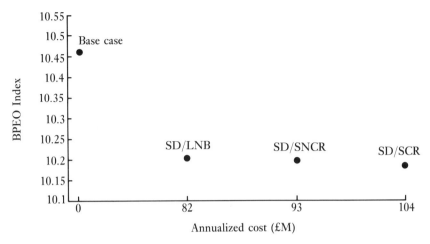

Figure 4.1 BPEO Index vs annualized cost. LNB; low NO$_x$ burners; SCR: selective catalytic reduction; SD: spray dry flue gas desulphurization; SNCR: selective non-catalytic reduction

assumed to propose the spray dry FGD plus low NOx burners on the grounds that to implement the BEO would involve excessive cost. A cost comparison was therefore required to evaluate the choice. The results are illustrated in Figure 4.1. They indicate that there is little reduction in BPEO Index for very significantly increased costs for the two most beneficial options. On this basis HMIP accepted the option of spray dry FGD plus low NOx burners could be justified as the BPEO/BATNEEC.

A number of other studies have been published, and these also provide useful procedural guidance.[3,4] A review procedure should also be established at the time of the BPEO study, particularly if more data will be needed to substantiate the selection at a later date. Finally, after implementation of the BPEO, a monitoring regime should be established to ensure that experience matches expectations. Throughout all of these activities an audit trail should be followed, assisting both in retrospective justification for the BPEO whenever it is required, and in updating the analysis from time to time. Local conditions, means of obtaining data, and technical, political and financial factors all need to be taken into account.

Another Assessment Method: A Life Cycle Approach

A review of Britain's legislation on the classification, packaging and labelling of dangerous chemicals required from September 1993 that substances dangerous to the environment must be labelled accordingly. They must also carry risk and safety phrases, with the latter indicating whether chemicals must be contained or recovered, releases to the environment avoided, and whether they should be regarded as hazardous waste. Not only legislation but also customers are driving such developments on labelling. One example of this is the requirement from the US market for certification that no ozone depleting processes have been involved in the manufacture of parts of a product through its life cycle. Alternatively, labelling that no such assurance can be given is required. Purchasing components in the world market has the result that products must be labelled as not complying, or compliance must be forced on suppliers. Here we see an impressive example of the supply chain pressures to which we have referred previously in this book. It also provides an example of where environmental pressures for certain improvements may not necessarily have an overall environmental benefit. Examples come from degreasing, for which aqueous products are not always effective in the industry, and can present major problems in non-destructive testing and assembly. Sometimes three cleaning processes have to be used where previously one was sufficient. Similar conflicts apply in relation to cutting fluids and balancing the overall benefits of sludge treatment and disposal against the costs of alternative techniques. Extremes of temperature to which the final product are exposed necessitate the development of organic solvent based paints rather than aqueous based ones for automobile manufacture. Increasing volatile organic emissions controls are resulting in pressures on the paint manufacturers to develop alternatives to meet these demands. Some of these conflicts are covered in the examples in Chapter 8.

Longer-term concerns result from emerging designs and technologies. For instance, precise structural requirements and grain orientation for many high temperature materials may mean that replacement rather than repair will be needed. In addition, a growing number of materials cannot be welded, but demand highly specialized, capital and energy intensive bonding processes.

All of these conflicts present difficulties for managers in making choices between options and suggest a clear demand for assessment methodologies to be further developed and agreed. They also indicate the need for environmental considerations to be a natural part of business decision-making, in the same way that financial issues are taken into account. What is the 'best' option from an environmental perspective? This question is not easily answered and is one of the taxing problems associated with integrated pollution control. Previously in this chapter we have considered one assessment approach. Another assessment method can use the technique of Life Cycle Analysis (LCA). This technique has received much attention recently, with variations of the concept being known as 'eco-balancing' or 'resource and environmental profile analysis'.

Basic principles

Definitions of LCA differ in detail. The Society of Environmental Toxicology and Chemistry (SETAC) definition is:

Life cycle analysis is an objective process to evaluate the environmental burdens associated with a product, process or activity by identifying and quantifying energy and materials used and wastes released to the environment, and to evaluate and implement opportunities to effect environmental improvements. The assessment includes the entire life cycle of the product, process or activity, encompassing extraction and processing raw materials, manufacturing, transportation and distribution, use/re-use/maintenance, recycling and final disposal.[5]

A second definition is:

Environmental LCA or product life analysis (PLA) are detailed studies of the energy requirements, raw material usage and water, air, and solid wastes generation of an activity, material, product or package throughout its entire lifecycle. Included are raw material sourcing, manufacturing/processing, distribution, use/re-use/ maintenance, and post-consumer disposal. The system under study is integrated in an input/output analysis and its material (raw material usage and waste generation) and energy flow are quantified. Based on this inventory, a final comparison among alternatives should be made, identifying opportunities for reducing energy requirements, raw material usage, emissions to water and air, solid waste generation and conserving natural resources (e.g. as part of a broader environmental auditing).[6]

Much initial work with LCA has focused on packaging materials, for which waste management and recycling have assumed great importance. The first LCA was claimed to have been done in 1969 for Coca-Cola beverage containers, while a second in 1970 compared polystyrene foam and moulded pulp meat trays. Compared with many products, packaging is relatively simple and so convenient for quantitative environmental analysis. However, as will become clear, LCA is not yet the universal panacea for identifying the best environmental option.

LCA plays a key role in the EU Eco-labelling scheme. The aim is to encourage manufacturers to introduce products which have a cradle-to-grave impact on the environment significantly less than other similar products. From the definitions it is apparent that the aim of doing LCA is to provide an objective means of quantifying the resource and energy consumption, together with the releases to air, land and water associated with the production, distribution, use and disposal of products. The results may be used to compare the overall environmental impact of products competing within the same market, and provide a basis for improvement programmes. However, life cycle analysis is still a developing tool, with no agreement on how best to do the analysis or to report its findings. Moreover, the essential input data are not always available or are overtaken by technological developments. Hence many commercial claims based on LCA have been severely criticized.

LCA surpasses traditional environmental impact assessments by producing an inventory of all material and energy flows from where resources are extracted from the earth, to either a point in the life cycle of the product, or the disposal of wastes back to the earth. It also offers an organization the means to:

- Reduce waste
- Conserve material resources and energy
- Continuously improve performance

By addressing these issues it serves not simply to provide good market information, but also focuses on the commercial needs of organizations.

Clearly, generating numbers alone serves no useful purpose; the data need to be interpreted and used in making policy decisions. Some refer to this stage in the process as 'eco-profile analysis'. This step may involve using an indicator substance from the overall system or aggregating the whole analysis into relatively few numbers, such as total material needs or total emissions to air, water and/or land.

Start by defining the system

The first stage of LCA is to define what you want to do, and early attempts at LCA have been subject to criticism through not defining precisely the system boundaries. To illustrate the difficulties in doing this, consider the following questions.

1   If wood is a raw material for your activities, is it a resource and therefore outside the system boundary, or is growing the trees a sub-system and part of the production life cycle?
2   Does fossil fuel winning start with exploration?
3   Is the disposal of waste to a landfill site the end of the boundary, or does the long-term management of the site need to be considered as part of the system?
4   Is capital equipment included? Indications suggest that the environmental impact of capital plant is relatively small in relation to that of products. The inevitable exceptions include transport, which has a relatively shorter life than other capital plant.
5   How are multi-output processes allocated? A process producing several products may have allocations made according to mass, energy value of the products or their capital value. Mass is convenient for products other than services, but may have limitations. Where the mass of a product is relatively low, but its economic value is high, as with a pesticide or pharmaceutical product, a mass allocation may associate much of the environmental effect to by-products rather than to the principal product.

The function is also important. Customers buy paints for surface coating, with features of coverage and longevity being important. These may be important features in comparing solvent based and aqueous based paints, rather than simply using mass or volume comparisons.

1 What geographical boundaries are to be used? International business activities make this a critical question.
2 What time boundaries are to be taken? Discounting future pollution is far more difficult than discounted cash flow for financial analysis.

The fact that some analyses will include different interpretations of the answers to these questions can make comparisons difficult, and have allowed invalid claims to be made about the environmental perfomance of certain products.

Produce a flow chart

After the boundaries have been defined, the life cycle analysis requires that each input in each process is traced back to resources taken from the environment, while outputs are followed to the final release into the environment. Effectively, a comprehensive flow chart is produced.

The inventory stage

The inventory stage is the process of identifying the energy, raw materials and wastes generated in the production, distribution, use and disposal of something. In principle this is a simple process, and data from an audit provides much of the information to fill in a balance sheet for the system.

Of course, there are often many subsystems, and so the overall effect is that the calculations to get overall mass and energy balances are complex. Large errors are possible, for example by omitting the secondary energy input to primary fuel production. Computer models for these processes carry out iterative calculations to produce a balance of inputs and outputs.

Where data are not readily available, suppositions and simplifications are necessary before a complete set of data is obtained. There are no agreed sets of data for producing the inventory, although a variety of databases are being compiled and are commercially available with LCA software packages. Unfortunately the databases may say little about the source of the data, which may vary from country to country. Aluminium production in the UK, for example, uses fossil fuel energy, while in Sweden the energy source is hydroelectric power. Likewise, there is a problem of whether to consider marginal, average or the best facility for a process. Correctly defining the system may help.

Unit processes make up the basic building blocks and may range from an aggregated process such as an oil refinery, or degreasing as a process step in metal coating. Consequently, it may be possible to analyse systems ranging in complexity from aggregated systems in a national economy to detailed studies comparing alternative production technologies for the same product, where unit processes are individual technologies. A typical database contains information on the inputs and outputs of many unit processes, including all material and utility consumptions, as well as all co-products and waste streams.

In general, mass balancing is done over the total releases to the environment and not over individual pollutants in the waste streams. Transportation impacts also need to be included, and must take into account not only the transport of goods for the production and consumption sectors, but also the fuel transport for transportation as well as goods transport in the energy winning and conversion sectors. The inventory is essentially adding up what goes in and what comes out of a system. Mass and energy balances are relatively straightforward. The problem comes in trying to classify the results.

Classification

The inventory is followed by a 'classification' stage in which the results of the inventory are translated into an expression of environmental loads or effects. The final stage is 'evaluation', in which classifications are compared to decide, for example, on the preferred method for doing something with the minimal impact on the environment.

There are many ways of combining the environmental impacts of all releases to land, air and water. For example, releases could be aggregated in terms of 'global warming' equivalents, or to water polluting potential and so on, but how do we weight an impact on global warming against one on ozone depletion in the stratosphere or on pollution of a lake? There is no agreement and a lack of standard guidelines as yet on how to achieve such classification on the harm that a product or system may cause to the environment. This problem is not unlike that addressed earlier in the chapter in relation to BPEO.

Life-cycle analysis is a tool still in its infancy, but growing interest in it owing to its potential usefulness merits the outline we have given here and the cautionary notes on its use. Several software packages are available.[7]

Practical Points for Action

- Develop a quantitative assessment procedure.
- Remember there may be many 'best' techniques to generate the 'best' environmental outcome.
- Interpret 'techniques' to include much more than the hardware of 'technology'.
- Identify targets, effects and pathways as key inputs to a BPEO analysis.
- Consider whether protection of humans also protects other species and the physical environment.
- Assess whether the BEO is practicable in your case.

References

1 DOE, *Integrated Pollution Control, a Practical Guide*, 1994, 16. The Department of the Environment and the Welsh Office, 2 Marsham Street, London, SW1P 3PY.

2 Based on a paper presented by HMIP to a seminar on 'Environmental and Economic Assessments for Integrated Pollution Control', Royal Horticultural Halls, London, 16 July 1993, and the Consultation Document 'Environmental, Economic and BPEO Assessment Principles for Integrated Pollution Control', HMIP, April 1994.

3 *Assessment of the Best Practicable Environmental Options for the Management of Low and Intermediate-level Solid Radioactive Waste*, HMSO, London, March 1986.

4 'Best Practicable Environmental Options for the Disposal of Non-radioactive Waste from the British Nuclear Fuels, Springfields Site', British Nuclear Fuels, Springfields, Lancashire, England, 1993.

5 J. A. Fava *et al.*, 'A Technical Framework for Life Cycle Assessments', Report of the workshop organized by the Society of Environmental Toxicology and Chemistry, Smugglers Notch, Vermont, August 18–23, 1990.

6 B. de Smet (Ed.), *Life Cycle Analysis for Packaging Environmental Assessment*, Proceedings of the specialized workshop, Leuven, 24/25 September 1990, Procter & Gamble Technical Centre, Strombeek-Beever, 1990.

7 Some LCA packages available include: the PIRA system (PIRA International, Leatherhead, UK); SimaPro (PRé, Amersfoort, the Netherlands) and IDEA (International Institute for Applied Systems Analysis, Laxenburg, Austria).

5

Monitoring

Monitoring is much more than mere measurement, and should not be confined to simply discharges and wastes. It should be the means by which effective operators satisfy themselves that the plant or activities in their charge are operating in the intended and most efficient manner. In Chapters 6 and 7 we show how measurement systems form an integral part of the environmental management system: monitoring is the precursor to intelligent and informed action. Traditionally much monitoring has been concerned with ensuring operational efficiency and only recently has it been recognized as *the* key means of measuring environmental performance and of maintaining good operational standards.

As the first sentence in this book reiterated, all too often operators have hidden behind a defence of not knowing—or caring about—the extent of pollution resulting from their activities. Fortunately, this attitude is rapidly becoming untenable. As we keep stressing, at all management levels pollution abatement is the aim as it is increasingly recognized that most pollutants are evidence of waste of resources with potential for loss of income, whether the pollutant is heat, a chemical or even noise (which could well arise from dry bearings or excessive pressure differentials, both of which could be costly in the long run!).

In this chapter we will concentrate on the monitoring of discharges and solid wastes. Other forms of in-plant monitoring can also have a profound effect on the pollution potential of a plant, but those aspects of the subject have been dealt with elsewhere. While monitoring may be required by the regulator to demonstrate that the plant is not in breach of conditions in an authorization, the responsible operator will, in any case, wish to know almost as much about discharges as about plant operations. The essential step is to establish all waste streams from the process and to understand how any existing pollution abatement equipment is working. There are often times when re-routing pipelines to treatment facilities, or even opening rarely used valves, can allow better use to be made of the existing facilities.

Next the manager requires to know the pollution loading of each waste stream and how it fluctuates within the range of the process operational parameters. The results of such studies can be well represented on a Sankey diagram. These representations are familiar in energy auditing (e.g. Figure 5.1). Similarly, the thickness of a pipeline on the diagram can represent the pollution load carried by the flow stream. A series of such diagrams can be a useful tool in representing improvements, whether achieved or planned.

Indeed, taking things one stage further, with efficient monitoring and suitable feedback into plant control, many of the plant fluctuations which can bedevil some industrial activities can be virtually eliminated. For example, the Edmonton (London) refuse incinerator at one time operated with a wide range of discharge levels for hydrocarbons and other undesirable combustion products. Installation of accurate equipment for continuously monitoring these

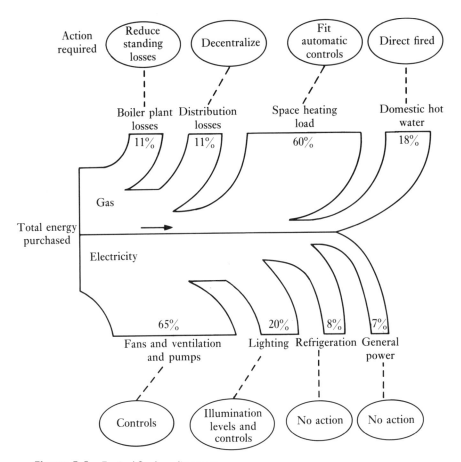

Figure 5.1 Typical Sankey diagrams

gases, and using the measurements to control combustion, allowed a ten-fold reduction in the variability of discharge levels, together with more efficient combustion in the incinerator itself. On a much smaller scale we can cite an example of a paint curing oven. Temperature monitoring indicated almost continuous operation of the oven at 215 °C whereas the paint specification required operation at 180 °C. Simply adjusting the temperature setting to specification and ensuring better control saved 1070 GJ (almost 300 000 kWh) of energy consumption each year, with the associated cost benefits. Operation at a lower temperature also reduces the risk of complaints from odour pollution by partial oxidation products, while burning less fuel produces less pollution from the combustion products. Modifying working practice to take advantage of continuous operation of the oven saved a further 865 GJ (240 000 kWh). In this example the failure was not in a lack of monitoring, but in lack of action based upon monitoring data. Monitoring alone serves little useful purpose; the aim should be to use the data for informed action.

In principle, monitoring can be undertaken in a variety of ways. Perhaps the simplest is by direct observation. The orange plume from a stack or the slime from an effluent pipe are indications that action needs to be taken, and the informed public will waste no time in alerting the company and the regulators to untoward events of this type. Similarly, odours, like noise, are readily detected by the senses, and regular sensory assessment may be part of the requirement for an authorization. However, many pollutants do not advertise their presence in such a direct manner. In these cases sophisticated analysis can be needed, sometimes working near the limits of detection, as for instance when measuring the low concentrations of dioxin in a stack gas discharge.

There may be few analytical techniques readily available for certain pollutants; in such cases it is likely that the regulatory authority will have specified which are acceptable and may well have laid down a detailed protocol for making the measurements. Then the operator needs to establish if the capability to make the measurements is available within the organization, or if a consulting analyst should be commissioned to undertake the work. If the analytical procedures demanded by the regulator are clearly beyond the capability of the operator—either in terms of the sophistication of the equipment required or because the cost is disproportionate to the benefit—then the operator should be prepared to make a case to the regulator for some relaxation. This could result in an alternative, and simpler, technique being accepted or, possibly, in the regulator accepting that his own independent monitoring programme will be adequate for the particular substance in question.

All too often the chemicals which pose risks or potential risks at low concentrations are also those which are most difficult to measure. Frequently discrete samples have to be taken, which are then sent to a specialized laboratory for analysis. This can take several days, or even weeks, and the results when they are obtained are too late for use in process or operational control. In such cases it is sometimes possible to identify a surrogate for the substance in question which is produced in a similar way, and is relatively easy to detect and measure. The surrogate then provides the instant qualitative indication of a problem long before the detailed analysis is complete. A simple example would be a change in pH of a liquid effluent, which in certain circumstances could result in the dissolution of a heavy metal from a sludge in contact with the liquid.

In cases where there are well-established analytical procedures which can be adopted by the operator at a relatively low cost, then there is no reason why the monitoring programme specified should not be implemented. In general it is better that operators develop the skills to undertake this work themselves so that they gain a feel for the levels of pollutants which the process is generating and how they fluctuate with other plant variables. Ownership of the problem also enhances motivation, but for small companies, particularly those without a technical or scientific base, it may be necessary to contract the work to a specialist company. If this procedure is adopted then the plant managers should, as a minimum, seek an understanding of the significance of the pollutant in the environment so that they are better placed to look for alternative ways of operation which could lead to a reduced environmental loading. As an example, changing gas temperatures in a combustion process, such as that described earlier, may well result in a reduction in discharges of pollutants as diverse as carbon dioxide or dioxins.

It is not our purpose to list all the analytical techniques which could be brought to bear in monitoring discharges. Every situation will have unique features and we recommend that, if appropriate techniques are not readily apparent, you first approach your regulator for advice, then a second approach could be to your professional association or a business partnership. For example, in the UK the Advisory Committee on Business and the Environment (ACBE) encourages the use of environment business partnerships to integrate environmental issues into small and medium business enterprises and several partnerships have been established.

Pollution control should not be a topic demanding great industrial secrecy and when there is a real analytical problem the club approach can not only bring more minds to bear on the problem and probably save costs, but give the companies concerned more power to agree cost-effective solutions with the regulators, or indeed in major cases with legislators. If this is not possible, then recourse to a professional consultant or analyst is called for. Unless the requirement is very complex it is likely that a number of organizations could satisfy your requirements: the laboratories of local government, central government, water authorities and consultants are all potential candidates and it can pay to shop around for the best deal in terms of cost and service. Currently, there is a surfeit of analytical capability in many developed countries, and for a reasonably long-term contract very competitive rates can be negotiated. The chief point to watch is that the analysis you commission matches what the regulator demands and what you need. If you are encouraged by a consultant to obtain more information then it should be for a good reason, for example, for better plant management or a better understanding of the process leading to the production of the pollutant concerned.

Two other points are important here. First, seek the advice of your analyst and never merely say 'analyse this'. Involve the analysts in the problem: if they understand it in detail they are likely to be able to provide a more appropriate solution. Secondly, the analyst's advice on sampling is paramount, for the validity of results depend on the validity of the sample.

The comments and advice above are of general application. There are particular features of solid and liquid bulk waste and of discharges to the air or water which need separate consideration.

Solid and Liquid Bulk Industrial Waste

Historically many bulk industrial wastes have been disposed of on the site where they were produced, using convenient excavations, boreholes, or sometimes simply as fill under new buildings. The sophistication now required to operate a dedicated disposal facility is such that the use of such disposal routes is rapidly diminishing. Even incineration which has been widely used for bulk reduction on sites is giving way to transport to central incineration facilities where economies of scale can justify the complex operational and pollution control systems now required by regulators and expected by an increasingly concerned public.

If waste is to be sent off the production site for landfill, incineration or, possibly, chemical treatment then it is no longer adequate to simply telephone a disposal contractor to collect it, and then forget it ever existed. In virtually all industrialized countries a continuing 'Duty of Care' is demanded.

Duty of Care

This legal obligation first requires an accurate knowledge of the chemical and physical nature of the waste in question. As the material is presumably stockpiled for some time before transit it should be possible to take representative samples for analysis and delay further action until the results are available. During this time it would be prudent to review the waste to check if there is any way of applying the five 'Rs' approach: reuse, repair, rejuvenate, refill, recycle. This will be amplified in Chapter 6. In particular, can the waste be recycled within the plant or elsewhere, or sold on as a by-product? Analysis of the waste is still required to take advantage of recycling opportunities. Fortunes can be made by those with the ability to turn a waste into a desirable product; the production of extracts like Marmite® from spent yeast in a brewery is a case in point. There is a cautionary note, however. First, the regulatory body requires the Duty of Care documentation to be complete. Then the user must declare in the documentation that a waste is being put into a product, and this may be a sensitive issue.

In Chapter 8, Section 2 we outline an elegant example of recyling within an Austrian mineral water bottling plant where virtually nothing is waste. Another simple example is waste polythene packaging from a supermarket chain being processed into bin liners and similar goods for resale in the supermarket.

If such investigations fail to identify a suitable outlet, then a disposal route has to found. First, the full analytical and physical documentation must be made available to a licensed carrier who needs to be satisfied that suitable vehicles can be utilized for transporting the material safely to a specified safe disposal (or incineration or treatment) outlet. However, in the UK this is not the end of the story. It remains a responsibility of waste producers to exercise the duty of care through to final disposal, and they should establish clear audit trails to demonstrate that they have done so. Table 5.1 summarizes these responsibilities.

This responsibility is undoubtedly more onerous for waste with a clear toxic potential or a recognized capability to cause environmental damage, but it applies to all wastes. The waste producer in particular has to ensure that comprehensive documentation identifies the constituents of the material, drawing particular attention to any potential hazards to workers, the public or the environment. The documentation should be in such a form, and with adequate copies, to accompany the waste through all stages to final disposal, and keep appropriate regulatory bodies appraised of its location and planned fate.

Table 5.1   The Duty of Care for waste

Do you have waste?	If so, you have a duty to stop it escaping. Store it safely and securely.
Do you use the waste disposal service of others?	Ensure that it is secure. Cover loose material contained in skips or vehicles. Identify whether your waste carriers need to be authorized. Check on their authorization. Does their authorization include your type of waste?
Have you completed the necessary documents?	A waste transfer note must include: a description of the waste type and amount; how it is contained; time and date of transfer; names and addresses of parties involved; details of licences or exemptions.
Is the waste description adequate?	You must provide enough detail for someone to handle the waste safely
Do you maintain records of waste transfers?	Copies of transfer notes and waste descriptions must be kept for two years.

However, the most important aspect of a duty of care relates to the final disposal itself. Not only is it incumbent on the waste producers to confirm that the disposal routes selected are adequate in principle, but they should also ensure that the waste actually follows routes specified. In the case of an environmentally significant waste this should involve inspection of the actual disposal facility. Indeed, it is best to track a specific waste load or loads, not only to ensure that disposal is consistent with your intentions, but also to track the paperwork and record keeping. Remember the cautionary example we gave previously: it is not unknown for the records to show that waste has been disposed of before it has been collected from the producer!

One way for a company without the resources—either technical or financial—to undertake such waste tracking is to join a club of producers who are all using the same facility. This enables them to commission a general audit of the disposal facility and share the cost, only meeting the full cost of any work undertaken specifically on their behalf. Commercial confidentiality can be ensured by making only the results of the general audit available to all club members (and to the site operator who will then have an opportunity to remedy any weaknesses identified). The company-specific work remains, or can remain, confidential to the company concerned.

It is essential that the results of all such tracking and audit activities are fully documented so that, if necessary, regulators can be satisfied that the duty of care has been dealt with in a responsible manner. While such documentation may not relieve the company of all responsibility in the case of an environmental incident involving the waste, doubtless a court would take full account of the manager's efforts to discharge a legal duty.

In the UK at present it is unlikely that a company would have a continuing liability for the consequences of the final disposal of a waste if an incident subsequently occurred, perhaps as a result of migration of leachate from a landfill site or simply from on-site spillage as the Eastern Counties Leather example in Chapter 8, Section 1 demonstrates. In other countries such a liability is continuing, indefinitely in the United States, as we have outlined in Chapter 2. This leads to major insurance problems, since either current insurance has to cover future events or insurance has to be maintained indefinitely, even after the site concerned has been closed. The insurance industry is currently grappling with this dilemma and doubtless a solution will result but at a price.

Liquid and Gaseous Discharges

While the taking of samples and their individual analysis is almost inevitable for the characterization of solid waste, there are major disadvantages for using the same approach for gaseous, and to a somewhat lesser extent for liquid, discharges. The real problem is that the discharges tend to be continuous while the plant is operating, and discrete samples can do little more than provide a snapshot of an instantaneous situation, perhaps days or weeks before. There can also be problems about taking a representative sample of a high volume effluent. These can be eliminated by using a succession of diluting weirs to take a truly representative proportional sample, but the costs will be high, particularly if the plant has to isolate discrete samples taken over time using a fraction collector system.

Even with such sophistication plant fluctuations, particularly during start-up or shut-down, can be easily missed, and there is little opportunity to use the monitoring results for operational control. To some extent these difficulties can be overcome in the case of a liquid waste by bulking the effluent in a holding tank and not sentencing it for discharge until the analytical results are available. The procedure is adopted for some wastes with a very high toxic potential, for instance in the nuclear industry, but the costs, both in terms of delay and finance, rule out such an approach in the majority of situations.

Nevertheless, regulators have traditionally relied on the taking and analysis of discrete samples—either by their own officers or by the operator—to check compliance with authorizations. One very strong argument in favour of such a sampling regime is that a sample can be split three ways: a tripartite sample. One is then available for the regulator to analyse, one for the operator, and a third can be held in case independent analysis should be required by a court or other judiciary body. Indeed, some legislation specifically demands such samples in support of any enforcement action.

Although for such reasons there may well be a continuing need for discrete sampling, bringing with it the ability to employ virtually any analytical technique under controlled laboratory conditions, there can be no doubt that the way ahead will be directed towards continuous monitoring whenever possible. Apart from the obvious advantages outlined earlier, continuous monitors bring other benefits. Whereas historically regulators have been content to limit their discharge conditions to a simple specification of concentration, now much more has to be controlled. Ultimately the objective of environmental regulation is to protect humans and their environment, and it is now recognized that a simple measurement of concentration may well be inadequate to do so. The operator can expect to work within mass concentration limits integrated over weeks, months and/or even a year! Continuous measurement is really the only way to meet such demands.

Furthermore, there may be environmental quality standards (EQSs) for the receiving medium—air or water. To satisfy any one of these it is not only necessary to be aware of the load which results from your own company's emissions, but it could be prudent to know the background levels resulting from other activities. Then, if an EQS is breached you may well be able to demonstrate that your contribution was not the last straw which broke the camel's back. Modern continuous monitoring systems give you this capability as we shall demonstrate.

Until recently anything other than the simplest continuous monitoring devices, for instance for pH, required highly sophisticated and expensive equipment. The current environmental pressures have, however, caused instrument manufacturers to seek cost-effective solutions to a wide range of continuous analysis demands. This, coupled with the miniaturization which comes from integrated circuitry and semiconductor detectors, is also leading to fundamental reductions in instrument system cost with a corresponding increase in reliability. Some systems which five years ago were moved around in a ten-tonne truck have now been replaced by hand-held devices which do the same job at a small fraction of the earlier cost.

It will only be a matter of time, and in our judgement a short time, before virtually all essential measurements (or perhaps their surrogates as described earlier) will be possible by continuous techniques. We will simply describe typical recent developments for monitoring discharges to air and to watercourses. We will also focus only on the measurement of emissions, since this is more directly related to operational control and regulatory requirements. However, measurements in the wider (ambient) environment are sometimes required for regulatory or other purposes. Detailed description of this wide field is beyond the scope of this book.

Monitoring of Discharges to Air

Discharges to air are normally measured using stack gas monitors. These are not without their problems. Many stacks are old and were not designed with monitoring ports or provision for access near a good sampling location—close to the point of discharge to atmosphere, for instance. Consequently climbing in hazardous situations may be required to take discrete samples. Even where access to a port is provided, great skill is needed to make sure the sample is representative and extracted isokinetically (i.e. sampling at the same flow rate as the gas flow in the absence of the sampler to ensure that gas flow patterns are not distorted: this can be an essential requirement for sampling dust or grit emissions). A large sample is required to obtain adequate material for detailed analysis and problems of settlement of dusts and chemical reactions of components have to be taken into account, together with the deleterious effects of the highly hostile chemical environment normally found in a stack.

The range of methods available for carrying out manual sampling and measurement of atmospheric emissions is wide, with a corresponding range of accuracies. The US Environmental Protection Agency has reviewed these and proposed a series of integrated, modular samplers linked together as a method known as the Method 5 train. This has much to commend it for those organizations choosing to depend on sampling and analysis. Such manual methods are tending to be used primarily as reference test methods for the alternative on-line instruments which are becoming more readily available.

When a simple sample cannot be taken, other techniques have to be used. For instance, for volatile organic compounds the organic component will normally be concentrated on an adsorbent, which could be made continuous by putting the adsorbent on a tape slowly moving past the sampling port. It can then be desorbed in a laboratory and analysed by very sensitive techniques like gas chromatography or mass spectrometry to characterize the chemical composition. Flame ionization and photoionization detection are other possible systems, but they can be liable to interference unless combined with gas chromatographic or similar separation techniques, and need careful and regular recalibration if the results are to be meaningful over time. Similarly, sampling onto a tape can be used as a method of collecting particulate matter for subsequent examination and analysis.

In general, manual methods should be used for the preliminary assessment of any emission whose composition is uncertain, as the choice of the most appropriate on-line detector will be influenced by the nature of the emission itself. There is such a great variety of techniques, and new ones are being developed so rapidly that it is impracticable to describe them fully here. The most important are summarized in Table 5.2, referenced in terms of the appropriate US or British Standard when appropriate.

Great improvements are now possible by the continuous measurement of many stack gas components from a bleed sample. A state-of-the-art environmental monitoring station is now a fully automated sophisticated laboratory for measuring and analysing a wide range of parameters. The self-contained station can be designed to require a minimum of maintenance and servicing, often by a specialist contractor so that the plant operator has no need to employ specialist staff. Digital control systems can accept data from a wide range of digital and analogue sensors providing hard copy data in a form satisfactory to regulators and management as well as output signals for process control or alarms if desired. It is even practicable to transmit results via a modem directly to central stations or to the offices of regulators.

Table 5.3 gives examples of the detectors and substances which can now be monitored continuously and reliably. While these and other substances can be

Table 5.2 Summary of typical standard sampling methods for emissions

Pollutant	Standard method	Comments
Particulates	UK BS3405:1983 US EPA Method 5	Isokinetic sampling
Oxides of sulphur	BS6059:1989 ISO7934 BS1756:Part 4	Hydrogen peroxide oxidation
Oxides of nitrogen	BS1756:Part 4	All oxides converted to nitrogen dioxide
Hydrogen chloride	EPA Method 28	HCl absorbed by H_2SO_4
VOCs	No standard	Adsorb on charcoal, etc.

Table 5.3 Continuous instrumental methods for emission monitoring

Ultraviolet fluorescence	Sulphur dioxide
Chemiluminescence	Nitrogen oxides
Infrared absorption	Carbon monoxide
Ulltraviolet absorption	Ozone
Flame ionization	Hydrocarbons
β radiation absorption	Dust

measured with stack systems there are still weaknesses in this type of measurement. The sensors are often in a very aggressive environment (high temperatures and corrosive gases) and as a result may have relatively short working lives. Cross stack systems where a beam is projected across a stack or a duct with a detector on the other side can sometimes deal with incomplete mixing and remove the system from the aggressive atmosphere. Cross stack monitors commonly use infrared beams to monitor for CO and NO, but normally they only give a qualitative measure of the emission, which has to be backed up with more quantitative techniques. Systems can also be used to measure particulate content by light scattering, radiation absorption or infrared techniques.

With all such systems calibration can be a problem. It is also easy to miss fugitive emissions, i.e. those emitted other than from the stack, for instance through oven or furnace doors, vents, leakages from chemical storage tanks and evaporation of volatile solvents. Emissions caused by wiping surfaces with a solvent-impregnated rag come into this category, as do those from pouring a liquid or powdery material from one level to another. These releases can account for a significant part of the total emissions from a wide variety of processes. Non-obtrusive, long path measurement offers a solution in such cases.

This technique employs a beam of optical radiation (usually infrared or near ultraviolet) as the actual gas sensor, and this is sent on a path anywhere from a few metres to tens of kilometres in length. The wavelength of the radiation can be selected so that the beam is selectively absorbed by the target gas under investigation and is not absorbed by other gases present in the path. The reduction in the intensity of the beam due to its passage through the target gas then gives a direct measure of its average concentration. Some of the gases which can be monitored virtually instantaneously in this way at the parts per million level are listed in Table 5.4.

Owing to the way measurements are made it is possible to scan across a site and detect not only the primary emissions, but also the fugitive emissions. Here the ability to detect a wide range of volatile organic compounds (including alkanes, alkenes, alkynes, aromatics and vinyl chloride) is of particular value, for instance at oil refineries or paint shops. By measurements around the site concentration profiles can be established and general atmospheric concentrations arising from neighbouring plants can be distinguished and allowance made for them.

Table 5.4 Options for long-path monitoring

Ultraviolet/visible	Infrared
Nitric oxide	Nitric oxide
Nitrogen dioxide	Nitrogen dioxide
Sulphur dioxide	Sulphur hexafluoride
Ozone	Ozone
Mercury	Ammonia
Benzene	Hydrogen chloride
Toluene	Carbon monoxide
Xylenes	Hydrogen fluoride
	Water
	Carbon dioxide
	Methane
	Nitrous oxide
	All volatile organic compounds

There are now several types of long range optical gas monitors available, some of which allow the operator to actually measure gas concentrations along the optical beam. Such 'range resolved' systems use lidar, the optical counterpart of radar to give the fullest information about the distribution of gas over regions several kilometres in extent and require only one location for the send and receive devices. The most common is differential absorption lidar (DIAL) which has been developed largely at the UK's National Physical Laboratory (NPL).

Path averaged long path monitors are somewhat simpler and they can use their own radiation sources or rely on ambient thermal or solar radiation. The passive monitors can be difficult to use in a quantitative way, but they can be extremely useful in identifying fugitive emissions for more detailed study by more conventional means.

On the other hand the active monitors are normally quantitative and can use laser or non-laser radiation. The latter can use a wide variety of detection techniques, including differential absorption, differential optical absorption spectrometry, wavelength modulation and Fourier Transform infrared systems. In principle, all can use topographic targets in which a small amount of radiation is returned to the monitor off any convenient solid object, thereby obviating the need for either separation of transmitter and detector to opposite ends of the beam traverse or a distant reflecting unit to return the beam to a detector close to the source. One such system is the infrared Hawk unit, which is a self-contained portable instrument (Figure 5.2), which can be tuned to monitor one gas at a time or a group of related gases, e.g. hydrocarbons. It is effective in monitoring CO_2, SO_2, CH_4, N_2O, NO_2 and propane. It can rapidly detect concentrations of a few parts in 10^9 and responds to changes in gas concentration within seconds. However, where practical it is best to use a mirror to return the beam or to have the source at one end of the path and the detector at the other.

(a)

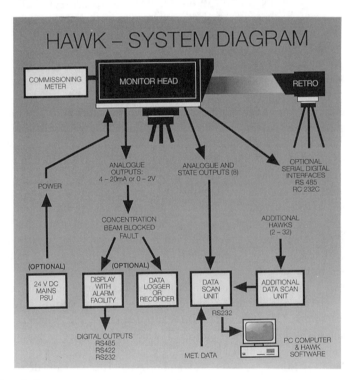

(b)

Figure 5.2 The infrared Hawk unit, a self-contained portable instrument for assessing discharges to air: (a) the equipment, (b) system diagram (Courtesy Siemens Plessey Controls Ltd)

Some idea of the sensitivity of these devices can be judged from tests made by the NPL in which the methane produced from buried waste on a landfill (or, indeed, by cattle in a field) and hydrocarbon leaks from pipelines have been pin-pointed. While devices of this type are expensive at present, there is no doubt that costs will fall as demand increases. In any case specialist companies now offer services whereby mobile equipment and operatives can be hired to carry out periodic surveys for operators or regulators.

Continuous Monitoring of Discharges to Water

Discharges to water have many similar characteristics to the atmospheric discharges we have just considered. It is possible to take discrete samples from within a discharge pipe or immediately after discharge from it. Alternatively, continuous monitoring from the pipe can be arranged for a number of substances. Finally, the receiving waters can be monitored to check on compliance with EQSs or to measure the build-up of a pollutant from several points or diffuse sources. All approaches have their place, but continuous monitoring should be undertaken whenever practicable, since the timing of water discharges can often be controlled by operators and pollution control officers cannot always be present to make or check discrete sampling.

Many systems for continuous monitoring are available, but what is needed for really effective control is a flexible system, immune from the risk of tampering but with the results immediately available to regulators for compliance checking and to operators for process control. One system which is currently gaining wide acceptance was developed by Wessex Water in the UK. It is capable of adaption for in-pipe monitoring (called Cyclops), for use as a floating system for mooring in a waterway (called Merlin, Figure 5.3) and as a transportable system for making continuous measurements on a river bank or elsewhere as the need arises (called Sherlock).

The systems work on the principle of analysing water *in situ* and at present are capable of measuring dissolved oxygen, ammonium ions, pH, turbidity, conductivity, salinity and temperature using probes which have automatic cleaning facilities. Other probes are being developed to analyse specific chemical species. Merlin is the most sophisticated. It is contained in a stainless steel bin, not dissimilar to a trash-bin. It can be anchored anywhere in a waterway. Sensor probes are mounted beneath the drum and the readings are stored in an internal data logger which transmits to a base station or other monitor units by short wave radio.

Alarms can be programmed to cause the units to take discrete samples (to support possible litigation, for instance) or to alert operators and regulators of an abnormal discharge. Any other units in a network can also be alerted by radio, so that they also take samples and build up a picture of the transit of the pollutant along a pipe or waterway.

(a)

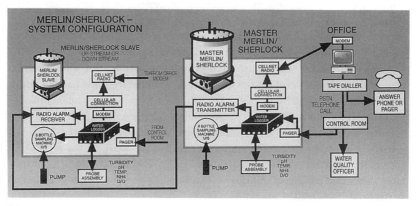

(b)

Figure 5.3 A continuous monitoring system for discharges to water: (a) the Merlin system, (b) system configuration (Courtesy Siemens Plessey Controls Ltd)

Noise and Odours

Both noise and odour pollution are highly subjective, familiarity tending to build up a natural tolerance. However, they can be of major concern to those living or working close to sources. Instruments are available to quantify noise levels, and they are directional and reliable. Whilst they can show changes in level as operational procedures are modified, and will demonstrate compliance or otherwise with statutory limits, they are not of great help in dealing with complaints, which are best handled by direct discussions and giving evidence that 'Best Available Techniques' are being used to ameliorate the disturbance.

Odours are even more subjective, and until recently the nose has been the most sensitive detector for many of the most disturbing smells, which have been assessed by panels of human 'sniffers' exposed to a common source. Recently there have been moves to develop reliable odour monitors using semi-conductor odour sensors. One such device provides a choice of 15 sensors which can be used to fingerprint an odour and then allow qualitative or quantitative assessments of change to be made, even of mixed odours.[1] Some of the applications where it can be used are:

- Food industry
  - Freshness of fruit and vegetables
  - Coffees, tobacco, wines, beers
  - Meat, fish
  - Product/packaging interactions
- Cosmetics/perfumes
  - Design of new cosmetics
  - Efficiency of deodorants
  - Quality control
  - Comparison between products
- Chemistry
  - Measuring paper odours
  - Measuring solvents from paint/plastics
  - Quality control of pharmaceuticals
- Polymers
  - Measuring general odour from PVC, etc.
  - Penetrability of odour through packs
  - Measuring odours in mineral water
- Environment
  - Olfactory fingerprints in works
  - Plant monitoring
  - Efficiency of odour eradication schemes

Data Availability

In the USA, Title III of the 1986 Superfund Amendments and Reauthorisation Act (SARA) insists that companies report data on all the pollutants they release to the environment. Under the UK Environmental Protection Act, 1990, monitoring data required by a regulatory body to demonstrate compliance with an authorization has to be made available to the public at local council offices and the offices of the regulatory body. The EC Directive on the Freedom of Access to Information on the Environment (Directive 90/313) similarly requires public authorities to make information available to individuals and businesses. It is therefore important to ensure that the data are clear and concise so that non-technical members of the public can appreciate their significance. Many yards of chart paper are of little use to the concerned inhabitant, and care should be taken to establish that adequate explanations of the significance of the measurements are available. Excellent examples of how detailed data can be expressed clearly and concisely are available in reports prepared by the nuclear industry (Nuclear Electric, Scottish Nuclear and British Nuclear Fuels). All are freely available and can be seen at local offices of HMIP in England and Wales and of HMIPI in Scotland. Following the example of the US EPA, HMIP have also now published the first of an annual series of National Emission Inventories consolidating the results of statutory monitoring requirements. With the back up of the detailed monitoring information they provide a thorough analysis of the industry's monitoring activities. We commend them to organizations outside the nuclear field.

Practical Points for Action

- Remember that monitoring is more than measurement.
- Understand the flow of pollutants through your plant and use monitoring results whenever possible for process control.
- Use continuous (and instantaneous) monitors whenever possible.
- Beware of other companies whose pollutants are released into the same environmental sink and which could set constraints on your own discharge levels.
- Ensure the 'Duty of Care' monitoring requirements are satisfied for solid wastes.
- Consider the technical and financial advantages of a 'club' approach to monitoring

Reference

1   Fox Odour monitor, Alrad Instruments, Alder House, Turnpike Road Industrial Estate, Newbury, Berks.

6

Pollution Prevention and Optimized Environmental Performance

In the earlier chapters we have explored in detail the factors which can influence a company's environmental performance. Now we will pull together many of the principles into means of optimizing production and environmental performance.

What is waste? Most of us may imagine we can define the word, but legally there are many terms qualifying wastes as 'controlled', 'hazardous' 'industrial', 'household', and so on. The specific details need not concern us here. It is sufficient to note that in the UK under the Control of Pollution Act, 1974, and Environmental Protection Act 1990 waste is:

> ... any substance which constitutes scrap material or an effluent or other unwanted surplus material arising from the application of any process.

From regulations made under the Environmental Protection Act 1990[1] there is a further qualification that 'waste means solid or liquid wastes or gaseous wastes (other than gas produced by biological degradation of waste)'. An encyclopaedic approach to classifying all types of waste is attempted through EU Directives.[2] Whether a material is a waste or a product may depend on the source and destination. For example, packaging waste from a large supermarket chain may be processed into dustbin liners and similar products for resale in the supermarket and elsewhere. In order to assist in distinguishing between wastes and products, OECD proposals have been made in the context of the Basel Convention on the Transboundary Movement of Hazardous Wastes. The following criteria should be considered.

- Is the material produced on purpose and/or prepared for specific uses?
- Does the material meet official or commercial product standards/specifications?
- Does the material normally have positive economic value?

- Is the material covered by commercial contracts in which the receiver purchases the materials from the generator/owner?

The first two of these are usually the crucial factors in determining whether a material is a product or waste, since the last two usually apply to wastes destined for recovery operations. The complexities of the definitions of waste need not be considered further here. More relevant is the determination from legislators to seek real reductions in waste volumes. Organizations must look at their wastes and cut down the quantities, and both command and control and economic instruments will be used to achieve these cuts. There is also the need for a 'Duty of Care' which, as described in Chapter 5, requires all reasonable steps to be taken to look after any solid waste you generate, to prevent its escape, and to prevent its illegal disposal by others.

'End-of-Pipe' Versus 'Pollution Prevention' Techniques to Deal with Wastes

With the broad social awareness of the consequences of poor waste management, the subject has become a technological problem in the sense that clean technologies are required to minimize waste production and even to avoid the generation of waste completely where possible. This accords with the legal pressures, such as those in the UK, which set objectives; first for the prevention of waste, then minimizing that which cannot be prevented, and finally rendering harmless the waste ultimately released to the environment. It may be argued that practical 'waste minimization' cannot be achieved as rarely are we able to identify the 'minimum'. Nevertheless the objective is sound, and other terms have been introduced which convey a little less precision, such as clean technology, waste reduction and eco-efficiency. The term 'cleaner production' was used by the United Nations Environment Programme. Some prefer the term 'pollution prevention' and this has without doubt replaced the concepts of pollution abatement or pollution control as the optimal strategy to deal with wastes. Even pollution prevention is not without criticism, for some have asked what does it embrace. Certainly it is true that 'end-of-pipe' control options prevent pollution reaching the environment, but these should never be the first line of attack on a problem. End-of-pipe treatments are reactive and selective. They are influenced by traditional conceptions about the way things are done and about control options, as well as representing an increasing cost to organizations and to the society in which they operate. Pollution prevention through cleaner production techniques is preventive and inherently safer, since potentially polluting wastes are eliminated at source. The solution is no longer purely technical, however, since the management role is increased (Figure 6.1 and Table 6.1).

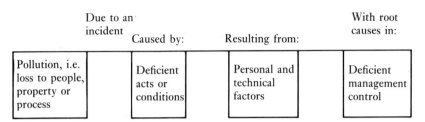

Figure 6.1   The management role in identifying causes of pollution problems

Table 6.1   Options for pollution control and pollution prevention

	Techniques
Pollution control	
End-of-pipe;	Authorizations
Add-on equipment for water and air pollutants;	Standards
Disposal of waste	Charges
	Subsidies
Pollution prevention	
Minor process changes;	Information
Integrated reuse and recycling;	Subsidies
Use of less harmful materials	Charges
	Threats of future legislation

From Table 6.1 it is evident that techniques to encourage pollution prevention are less persuasive than those aimed at control, but the integrated pollution management system we are advocating embraces prevention as a key step, while the integrated pollution prevention and control concept (IPPC) from the EU makes the integration explicit.

The general approach to waste management taken by the Royal Commission on Environmental Pollution provides a useful guide and has most recently been stated in its 17th Report.[3] The Commission's view is that waste management must be based on a four-stage decision procedure:

1   Avoid creating wastes wherever possible.
2   Where wastes are unavoidable, recycle them if possible.
3   Where waste cannot be recycled in the form of materials, recover energy from them.
4   When the preceeding options have been exhausted, use the best practicable environmental option to dispose of the wastes.

The sequence must be followed with care, however, as the problems with the German packaging ordinance introduced in Chapter 3 illustrate. The collection of waste packaging for recycling exceeded the market capacity, and incineration with energy recovery is not an option. Hence wastes have been exported to other 'disposal' routes. Other countries have learned from this and include incineration with energy recovery as acceptable 'recycling' for at least domestic packaging. Thus, the French government packaging decree, effective from January 1993, chose not to set specific targets for recycling packaging waste, but used the concept of 'valorization'. This embraces recycling, material reuse, composting and notably incineration with heat recovery.

Among the many definitions, wastes have been called 'resources misplaced in time', and this is reflected in a hierarchical structure of the options for dealing with waste. This structure recognizes that waste management means more than careful disposal; we are really concerned with the efficient management of resources.

A typical scheme is based on environmental protection considerations, but is influenced by social demands and political pressures as appear through legislation. Increasing costs of disposal are also playing a major role in changing attitudes to waste and are working with the legal pressures to encourage control.

Waste Audits

Guidance notes issued in the UK under EPA1990 suggest a waste audit for new plant according to the scheme in Table 6.2. It will be noticed that this develops from the principles of the BPEO concept introduced in Chapter 3.

Table 6.2   A Waste audit scheme

Assessment overview –	Summarizes overall assessment procedure
Programme organization –	Records key members of firm and its organization
Assessment and evaluation team make-up –	Lists assessments required and team member responsibilities
Process information –	Checklist of useful process information to look for prior to assessment
Input materials summary –	Names, supplies, hazardous properties, cost, delivery, shelf-life and possible substitutes
Product summary –	Hazardous components, production rates, revenues and other information about products
Individual waste streams –	Generation rate, hazard, method of treatment
Waste stream summary –	Collate waste stream information used to prioritize waste streams for assessments
Option generation –	Transforming to generate methods for treatment
Option description –	Summarize options generated
Options evaluation by weighted sum method –	
Technical feasibility –	Technical evaluation of options generated
Cost information –	Detailed capital and operating cost for economic evaluation
Profitability –	Payback, Net Present Value

Existing plant should follow a similar audit to quantify wastes and to derive a schedule for waste reduction. Too many organizations do not know what their wastes are costing them, with the result that there is little motivation to do something about them.

Following the sequence of events in Table 6.2, a prioritized set of options will emerge as:

1 Newer and cleaner processes
2 Reduction and recycling techniques
3 Treatment (end-of-pipe) options

This is the hierarchy which should be followed, but for practical application it may be expanded as shown in Table 6.3. The opportunities for minimizing waste and preventing pollution are limited only by the boundaries of imagination, invention and innovation, but identifying them may be assisted by a systematic approach.

The concept of auditing which we introduced in Chapter 3 provides a formal procedure for gathering the technical and economic data necessary for implementing a waste minimization programme. A team offers a wider range of experience, knowledge and problem appreciation than an individual can provide, but the size of the organization will influence this decision. However, the team leader or individual must have the authority to complete the task.

The work starts with collection of the types, amounts, compositions and sources of all waste streams of gases, liquids and solids. Existing background data, plant surveys, measurements and calculations combine to provide this information. Much of the background information needed is usually available, and is an obvious starting point. Table 6.4 provides a checklist on these background sources. Information on the activities carried out, layout on the site, waste-stream generation and the costs associated with those wastes should be available.

From this information it is usually possible to prepare a general flow diagram and perhaps a material balance for each system or sub-system and Sankey diagrams as shown on page 81. The flow diagram should clearly identify the sources, types, amounts and concentrations of each waste stream. Balancing the system flows in these diagrams to better than 10 per cent is often adequate. Where gaps or discrepancies are revealed, these serve to highlight information deficits from the site survey and the need for additional measurements.

The survey itself serves to confirm background data and to fill in the gaps in knowledge. Each stage in the activities must be examined from receipt of raw materials and other resources at the site to dispatch of the final products and wastes from the site. Some examples of losses in production areas are indicated in Table 6.5.

Table 6.3 Practical pollution prevention and control

Minimization at source				Recycling onsite/offsite		Control of releases
Product change	Process change	Input material	Technology	Use/reuse	Reclaim	
Substitute product	Good housekeeping procedures	Input material	Technology	Return to process	Recover material	Can waste be destroyed
Conserve product		Purification	Process change	Use as raw material for another process	Process as by-product	Can environmental hazard be reduced?
Change components in product	Employee training	Substitution	Better controls			Can containment be considered?
	Inventory control	Use of harmful materials	Change in operational settings			Is dispersal an option?
	Spill/leak prevention		Automation			
	Waste stream segregation		Change equipment piping or layout			
	Material handling		Conserve energy			
	Logistics		Conserve water			

First ————→ ACTION SEQUENCE ————→ Last

High ————→ relative desirability for environmental protection ————→ Low

Table 6.4　Background information for the audit

Process data
Site layout
Flow diagrams
Sewer layout
Purchasing records
Safety data sheets, e.g. COSHH forms
Operating manuals for processes
Water consumption data
Operating schedules
Production records

Waste information
Authorizations and licences
Monitoring data
Waste inventories for disposal routes
Details of enforcement notices
Location of waste collection and storage points
Details of pollution control plant
Operating manuals for pollution control plant

Financial data
Water charges
Effluent charges
Solid waste disposal costs
Costs of on-site treatment
Details of waste management contracts
Other information
Current waste minimization practice
Information from previous audits

Table 6.5　Examples of sources of loss

Area		Possible waste generated
General	Specific	
Material reception	Loading bays; pipelines in; receiving areas	Packaging; damaged containers; spills; leaks; reject materials
Stores	Tanks, silos, storerooms, drum storage	reject materials; surplus materials; spills; leaks; damaged containers
Production	Melting; baking; washing; coating; machining; mixing, etc.	Wash water; sweepings; additives; lubricants; solvents; residues; filters; leaks
Services	Offices	Paper; printing chemicals, etc.
	Laboratories	Chemicals; samples; disposable apparatus; containers
	Garages	Lubricants; filters; batteries
	Power plant	Fly ash; slag; chemicals; lubricants

Measurements are needed to provide data lacking from the initial survey. Typically each waste stream should be characterized by information on:

- Source
- Physical and chemical characteristics
- Amount
- Rate of generation, e.g. kg per unit of product or service
- Variations in rate of generation
- Potential for contamination or variation in quality
- Handling, treatment and disposal
- Cost of handling, treatment and disposal

Seasonal or production variations may make it necessary to make measurements over long or intermittent time periods.

The next stage is to identify, evaluate and select waste minimization techniques that may apply to the site under study. Whether quality circle, brainstorming or computer model techniques are used, all tend to involve the principles mentioned previously, namely:

- Listing waste streams
- Identifying techniques for minimizing each waste stream
- Evaluating each option from technical, economic and best practicable environmental option viewpoints
- Selecting the best option for each stream.

As part of the evaluation, the now familiar hierarchy should be followed to minimize both the waste and the environmental liability. The major causes of waste in processes are summarized in Table 6.6, while Table 6.7 gives some examples of practical improvements.

A full economic analysis should be carried out on each option considered. The financial analysis should include not only the costs of implementation (capital, installation, operating and maintenance) but also the financial benefits

Table 6.6 Causes of waste

Quality:	defects, rejects, reworks, revisions, unnecessary high standards, not defining criteria for success
Product design:	too complicated or not well developed
Quantity:	producing or supplying more or less than the customer requires
Time:	provision too soon or too late for the customer's needs
Distance:	transporting information, material or people further than necessary
Organization:	aiming to excel in function rather than procedures
Suppliers:	failing to involve and interact with them
People:	failing to allow people to give their optimal performance, in particular by failing to communicate objectives and to promote understanding

Table 6.7 Specific examples of waste reduction in practice

Source	General waste characteristics	Waste management practice	
		Current best	Minimization
Boilers for space heating and process plant	Combustion gases	Combustion controls, gas cleaning	Reduced need for energy, increase efficiency
Production fails to meet specification	Returned goods	Crush/shred, landfill, incinerate	Match production and quality to demand
	Solvents	Rework into product, incinerate	Increase efficiency, Quality Assurance
	Solids	Disposal, segregate for resale	Incinerate with heat recovery
	Seepage/leaks	Clean-up, preventive maintenance	Increase training and preventive maintenance

from more efficient operation, lower waste and therefore reduced disposal costs. Remember, however, that while some factors such as capital and operating costs or insurance premiums are easily expressed in monetary terms, it may not be possible to put a financial value on other, equally important aspects such as regulatory compliance, community relations and your organization's environmental image.

Many studies have identified lack of information as one reason for organizations failing to apply pollution prevention. Information is increasingly available from national and international sources, such as the Paris office of the UN Environmental Programme and Department of Trade and Industry in London, as well as trade and industry networks. Some examples are cited in the case studies. Yet another example of an information source is the Vendor Information System for Innovative Treatment Technologies (VISITT) developed by the US Environmental Protection Agency and introduced in Chapter 3.[4] VISITT provides current information on innovative treatment technology for the remediation of hazardous waste sites. The VISITT database is provided in the form of PC software and Figure 6.2 illustrates a typical screen.

Identifying Ways for Minimizing Waste

Various schemes have been proposed to aid in the identification of waste minimization opportunities. Not all may seem appropriate to a single organization, and so we suggest several approaches.

Practise good housekeeping

Perhaps the simplest approach is to examine everything in terms of the key words 'Time, Level and Efficiency'. Ensure that equipment operates for the

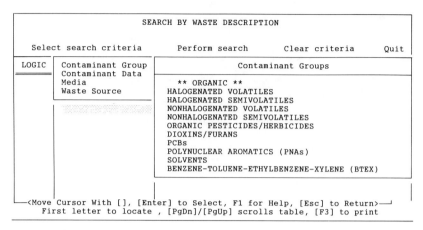

```
                      SEARCH BY WASTE DESCRIPTION


    Select search criteria        Perform search      Clear criteria     Quit

  ┌─────────┬─────────────────────┬─────────────────────────────────────────┐
  │ LOGIC   │ Contaminant Group   │           Contaminant Groups            │
  │ ═══════ │ Contaminant Data    │                                         │
  │         │ Media               │    ** ORGANIC **                         │
  │         │ Waste Source        │    HALOGENATED VOLATILES                 │
  │         │                     │    HALOGENATED SEMIVOLATILES             │
  │         │                     │    NONHALOGENATED VOLATILES              │
  │         │                     │    NONHALOGENATED SEMIVOLATILES          │
  │         │                     │    ORGANIC PESTICIDES/HERBICIDES         │
  │         │                     │    DIOXINS/FURANS                        │
  │         │                     │    PCBs                                  │
  │         │                     │    POLYNUCLEAR AROMATICS (PNAs)          │
  │         │                     │    SOLVENTS                              │
  │         │                     │    BENZENE-TOLUENE-ETHYLBENZENE-XYLENE (BTEX) │
  │         │                     │                                         │
  └─────────┴─────────────────────┴─────────────────────────────────────────┘
  └─<Move Cursor With [], [Enter] to Select, F1 for Help, [Esc] to Return>─┘
         First letter to locate , [PgDn]/[PgUp] scrolls table, [F3] to print
```

Figure 6.2   An illustrative screen from the VISITT database

minimum time, at the right level (of temperature, flow, etc.) and at optimum efficiency. An application of this approach can be taken from energy auditing during which these three concepts should be borne in mind while inspecting the site. Some examples of their application are given in Table 6.8.

Table 6.8   Time level and efficiency criteria: examples from the energy audit

Time	
Is equipment operating when it could be off?	Lights on
	Personal computers on
	Equipment on standby
	Exhaust ventilation with no production
Level	
Are control levels correct?	Steam pressure
	Lighting
	Compressed air pressure
	Furnace temperature
	Water flows
	Refrigeration set too low
	Water temperature too high
	Room thermostat too high
Efficiency	
Is equipment used to best advantage at all times?	Lighting clean
	Combustion efficiency
	Minimal air entrainment in ventilation
	No dust on ventilator/heater grilles
	Insulation
	Clean windows
	Design scale and type of activity to minimize waste
	Recycle waste inevitably produced

Table 6.9   Good housekeeping

Process plant and services	Typical payback period (years)
Turn off idle equipment	0
Improve production scheduling	0
Improve maintenance of heating equipment	0.5
Improve controls on plant	0.75
Insulate steam pipes, hot water pipes, hot air ducts (including joints and flanges)	0.75
Improve insulation on kilns and furnaces	1
Superior boiler maintenance and controls	1
Improve compressed air system, repair leaks, duct air from outside, etc.	1
More efficient lighting, better lighting controls	1–2
Space heating: improve/adjust controls, e.g. thermostat, time clock	0.5
Control heat loss through doors, loading bays, etc.	0.5

Often remedial measures require no expenditure, while others may require minor and a few even major expenditure. Payback can be rapid for essentially good housekeeping steps (Table 6.9).

More creative solutions

Another approach[5] suggests that throw-away society may be transformed in the future by the five 'Rs': reuse, repair, rejuvenate, refill and recycle. A more searching analysis of 'the way we've always done it' involves a series of key questions starting with 'what is accomplished?' This should be followed by finding out why and how it is done and what alternatives are available. Perhaps the activity is unnecessary, could be avoided or modified in terms of the 'level' of temperature, time, quantity, for example. Different materials, equipment or methods should all be examined in relation to why the activity is carried out.

A technique for generating creative solutions to environmental problems uses a set of key 'A' words (Table 6.10).

When we turn to more sophisticated schemes for identifying waste reduction opportunities, we return to the environmental audit idea, and one successful

Table 6.10   Creative solutions for pollution prevention

Alternatives	What can be substituted?
	What can be done instead of current practice?
Associations	What combinations can be advantageous?
Adjustments	What adjustments are possible?
Alterations	Can form or quality be changed?
	Consider size, weight, strength, speed
Applications	What new applications are possible?
Avoidance	What can you do without?
Arrangement	Can you change parts, order, layout or sequence?

START WASTE PREVENTION

Planning and Organization

1. Secure management commitment
2. Set up an assessment organization
3. Set overall prevention goals
4. Overcome hurdles
5. Carry out pre-assessment

ASSESSMENT:

---

1. Collect data on company and processes
2. Set priorities
3. Select people for assessment teams
4. Inspect the site
5. Generate options
6. Select options for further study

FEASIBILITY ANALYSIS:

---

1. Technical evaluation
2. Economic evaluation
3. Environmental evaluation
4. Select options for implementation

IMPLEMENT:

---

1. Arrange funding for feasible options
2. Intallation
3. Evaluate results
4. Initiate ongoing prevention programme

SUCCESSFUL WASTE PREVENTION PROJECT

Figure 6.3   Principles of the PRISMA pollution prevention route

approach to preventing waste and reducing emissions is the PRISMA project in the Netherlands.[6] This project identified many cost-effective waste reduction opportunities in a variety of different organizations including a bus service company, various metal fabricating processes and food production. The essential features of the PRISMA route are set out in Figure 6.3.

The PRISMA model was subsequently proposed for the Aire & Calder Project introduced in Chapter 3. This was one of the first co-ordinated waste minimization projects in the UK, dealing specifically with releases to a single river basin. Eleven participating companies started the first of three phases of the programme in 1992. In Chapter 5 we stressed the importance of monitoring ('you cannot manage what you cannot measure') and the companies started the study by improving their monitoring of water use and effluent discharges. This allowed baseline data to be established, improvement targets to be set and progress towards the targets measured. The second phase involved auditing the processes at each site to determine their contributions to resource use and effluent loads, while the final phase involved identifying waste reduction opportunities. To reiterate from Chapter 3, within one year, over 400 waste reduction opportunities had been identified in the 11 companies, and of this total some 20 per cent were good housekeeping while 60 per cent were operational changes. Only 20 per cent involved major changes in products or processes. A similar programme, Project Catalyst, was based in Merseyside in the UK. Over 500 waste reduction opportunities were identified in 11 organizations drawn from a wide spectrum of businesses. Financially, these opportunities were worth over £4 million to the organizations, while the environmental benefits included massive reductions in wastes to landfill, in liquid effluents, in discharges to air and in water consumption. Many waste reduction measures cost nothing to implement, such as ensuring that water supplies were not left on unnecessarily.

Further examples of solutions to pollution problems are to be found in the examples in Chapter 8. Remember that your application of best practice may offer commercial opportunities, not only in terms of cost savings and competitive advantage, but also as technology transfer business opportunities.

Practical Points for Action

- Are you aware of your duty of care for solid waste?
- Have you prepared material and energy balances as part of your waste audit?
- Know your waste routes, i.e. where wastes come from and where they go.
- Prepare flow diagrams.
- Determine what your wastes are costing you.
- Critically evaluate what you are doing, why you are doing it and how it is done. Are there alternatives?
- Identify examples of best practice by looking at demonstration projects.
- Have you applied the waste management heirarchy?
  - Avoid creating wastes wherever possible: look at cleaner processes.
  - Where wastes are unavoidable, recycle them if possible.
  - Where waste cannot be recycled in the form of materials, recover energy from them.
  - Where the above options are impracticable, use BPEO to dispose of the wastes.

References

1   Environmental Protection (Prescribed Processes & Substances)(Amendment) Regulations 1992 (SI 1992 No. 614).
2   EC Framework Directive (91/156/EEC) and Directive on Hazardous Waste (91/689/EEC).
3   Royal Commission on Environmental Pollution, 17th Report, *Incineration of Waste*, HMSO, London, 1993.
4   VISITT. Vendor Information System for Innovative Treatment Technologies, US EPA, Office of Solid Waste and Emergency Response Technology Innovation, Washington DC, EPA/542/R-92/001, 1994.
5   *The Environment: A Business Guide*, ACBE (a joint DTI/DoE initiative). DTI London, 1993.
6   *PREPARE Manual. Part I: Manual for the Prevention of Waste & Emissions; Part II: Choosing for Prevention is Winning; Part III: Business Examples with Waste Prevention*, Ministry of Economic Affairs, The Netherlands, June 1991.

7

Selling the Case

In Chapter 2 the changing nature of public opinion and pressure on environmental issues were presented as constraints on organizations. Unfortunately, technological developments are often associated with concerns among staff and the wider community that there may be risks to health or the environment linked with the new technology. Organizations need to exist in harmony with those living and working in the communities in which they operate. Community relations are therefore a key part of the environmental management function, with the aims of giving the public a better understanding of the operations of an organization, and responding positively to expressions of public concern. Developing from the crucial role of public opinion, it will be recalled from Chapter 2 that the CERES Principles included communication as a key factor among its guidelines for business, while in Chapter 3 we discussed BS7750 which includes publishing results of reviews and making information available to interested parties.

Increasingly, legislation includes provisions for communication to the public and others through information placed in public registers. This trend of increased communication on environmental issues will continue through legal pressures, such as those from the European Union, but should not be perceived as a threat. Rather it is an opportunity to build up good relations and to provide a basis of understanding that will stand an organization in good stead should environmental problems arise.

Communication to employees is essential, not only as part of the staff training and motivation programme, but also to enlist the support of staff in communicating to the general public of which they and we are a part. At all stages of communication there are a number of issues to be addressed. Within the organization, commercial sensitivities, company attitudes and site/process interactions need to be considered. Interactions with regulators may relate to inquiries, consent applications or appeals, while the public often want more general information. It is important to recognize the different attitudes and sensitivities of the various audiences.

It is worth noting the findings of a survey in Scotland on sources of information on environmental issues.[1] Television is the principal source of information on environmental matters for most people (72 per cent), followed by newspapers (46 per cent). Over half wanted to know more and felt that too little information was available, but considered central government (43 per cent) and industry (19 per cent) least trustworthy. More faith was placed in information from environmental organizations (57 per cent) and scientists (23 per cent). A similar pattern in the sources of information emerges from the USA, with 75 per cent of respondents gaining information from television news, 65 per cent from newspapers and 61 per cent from TV magazine programmes. Business sources accounted for only around 11 per cent of the information.[2]

There are clear messages in these findings for communication on environmental issues. Develop good relations with the media and local organizations, and try to develop trust by the community in your own information. Many communication systems are available to an organization (Figure 7.1). Some are impersonal, involving documentary and similar media, while others involve personal communication. For effective communication we need a feedback

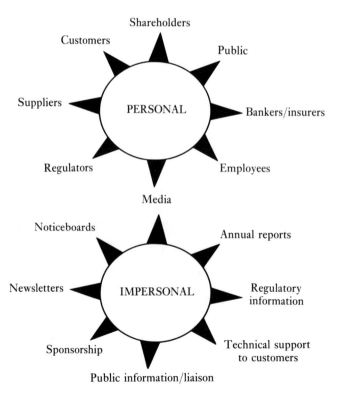

Figure 7.1   The cardinal points of communication

loop to repeat the process until there is mutual understanding, and so it is essential to reinforce impersonal routes of communication through personal ones.

A Technical Report from the UNEP Industry and Environment Office[3] made it clear that there is no single 'recipe for success'. In this chapter we explore some ways of achieving the goal of good communication on environmental performance, and examine some of the pitfalls.

First let us examine some problems of communication. The concept of risks involves interactions across many domains of the environment, and despite massive financial investment, political action and steady improvements in health, safety and the quality of life, technology is still perceived as a threat by many. The social structures and processes of risk experience, the resulting repercussions on individual and group perceptions, and the effects of these responses on community, society and economy have been termed 'the social amplification of risk'.[4]

Signals about a risk may emerge from direct personal experience or through receiving information; these signals may be amplified by social and individual interactions which include the scientist conducting a technical risk assessment and communicating it, the news media, pressure groups, opinion leaders within social groups, personal networks and public agencies. We have seen that some of these amplification modes are more trusted than others, and there is the added problem that information may be incomplete or may become distorted. Therefore, the amplification process may result ultimately in effects such as:

- Enduring perceptions and attitudes against technology
- Impact on business sales, property values and economic activity
- Political and social pressure
- Changes in the perception of the risk through feedback
- Changes in education and training
- Social disorder such as protesting or even sabotage
- Regulatory changes
- Impact on other technological advances, e.g. low public acceptance or trust

The impacts may spread further to other groups, locations or generations, and the process has been likened to the ripple effect when a stone drops in a pond. We have seen several examples of risk amplification during recent years. The business impact of benzene contamination of Perrier water, the salmonella problem in eggs and the BSE disease of cattle and its impact on the beef market are three specific examples. At the extreme, the consequences of nuclear accidents at Three Mile Island and Chernobyl have placed in doubt the future of nuclear power itself. Remember that reputations your organization spent years building can be destroyed in a moment, along with its commercial value.

More directly related to environmental pollution are concerns over waste disposal operations and many acronyms have emerged in response to such issues. NIMBY (not in my back yard), LULU (locally unacceptable land use), NOPE (not on planet earth) and BANANA (build absolutely nothing anywhere near anyone) are familiar examples.

External Communications

Much has been written in recent years about communicating with the public on pollution and other risk issues and different perspectives have emerged. One relatively simple view identifies three options: ignore public perceptions, try to change them or work with them. A broader analysis[5] considers a spectrum of approaches (Figure 7.2) ranging from the one-way telling to the two-way sharing of information and means to encourage participation by the whole community, of which the organization is itself a part. Opponents to the latter approach argue that public pressure groups can stop even low risk but unpopular projects, using emotive arguments to generate political pressure. However, sharing responsibility to work towards acceptable solutions to environmental problems surely depends on sharing information.

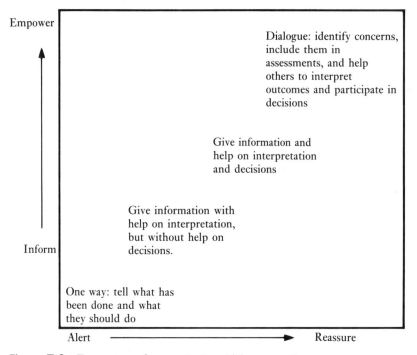

Figure 7.2   The spectrum of communication with the community

These ranges of communication possibilities illustrate the importance of defining the goal. Do you want to make people aware of a risk of which they are ignorant, or has a situation changed and made the risk different from hitherto? Do you want people to seek information to enable them to take action themselves, perhaps for protection in the unfortunate event of an accidental major release of pollutant, or do you want them to participate more in the decision-making process? In some cases, information is needed to enlist support for a narrowly defined objective such as damage control, while in others the objective is to overcome unfounded opposition to a proposed development. The two-way exchange of information allows an organization to gain a perspective of how 'outsiders' view it and what issues are considered important to them. Communication with pressure groups, regulators and media representatives can identify what they regard as significant issues, and how those issues fit into the whole life cycle of the organization's activities.

Yet another objective may be to gain informed consent to a proposal by public empowerment. A key element is to define the partners in communication. The upper part of Figure 7.1 identified many of the audiences, and each of these may require and impart distinctly different types of information, ranging from the detailed technical appraisal to the general outline. For the following discussion we will broadly categorize the various target groups into community communication and staff training and awareness.

Communicating with the Community

In Chapter 2 the constraints of the market-place and the pressures of public opinion were introduced. Of course the two are inextricably linked and can have a profound influence on the activities of an organization.

> The marketplace has the means 'to bring to the court of public opinion those who do not fulfill their commitments'
>
> (R. Stevens, Environmental Affairs Manager, Du Pont, and Vice-Chairman of ICC working group on sustainable development: in *ICC Business World*, March 1992)

The community is not just that around your perimeter fence, but increasingly further afield. Nevertheless, the local community is an important target group for public information, not only when consents to operate are being sought, but also as a continuing demonstration of social responsibility and path to competitive advantage. Open communication with the community leads to better understanding of mutual concerns, and codes of practice recognize this. For example, the Responsible Care described in Chapter 3 commits members of the Chemical Industries Association to managing their activities so that they present an acceptably high level of protection for the health and safety of employees, customers, the public and the environment. Responsible Care 'opens up ... industry to our neighbours so that they feel more comfortable with us. As their fear of the unknown disappears, we gain greater acceptability in our communities'.[6]

Critics argue that the programme requires no more than a pledge from the Chief Executive with no action resulting from policies. Making the programme a condition of CIA membership has without doubt increased support, but this alone cannot bring about commitment. While reports have not denied lack of action by some, attitudes are changing. Improved performance to secure a licence to operate, peer pressure from other business leaders, and the link with total quality are all supporting the programme.

A variety of ways for an organization to communicate environmental issues to the community has been used. Letters, fact sheets and brochures sent to homes in the neighbourhood together with briefings and meeting with local representatives can start the communication process and initiate a dialogue among interested parties. Many organizations also publish information on their environmental activities and performance measurements in magazine format. One example of this is BP Chemicals at its Kingston-on-Hull site. First published in 1991 as a tabloid newspaper publication, *The Green Challenge* described the pollution created by the BP Chemicals' site and explained the plans for dealing with these problems. Despite reported reservations by some within the corporate organization, the publication was held up to all of the company's sites worldwide as a model of how openness should operate. It also served as a model on communications for other parts of the organization. Subsequent issues included explicit detail on 58 substances released from the site into the environment in quantities down to 1 tonne per year, as well as details on targets to reduce these emissions. The 1993 issue reported progress on target to cut its pollution by the specified deadlines, but also stated:

- Staff at all levels will have waste reduction as high in their priorities as profitability and safety.
- The public will have access to information about the environmental impact of all the factory's processes.

A two-way communication process is also explicitly part of company policy, which includes the statement that the group will:

> Communicate openly with those living or working in the vicinity of company facilities—ensuring that they understand its operations and that the company understands the community's concerns.

Community views are included in the newspaper, and it is noteworthy that a 1993 public opinion survey revealed that while the factory was listed as the main polluter, there was significant and growing trust, and a rising opinion of its environmental performance.

A similar, but smaller publication from National Westminster Bank plc provides information on its environmental responsibility programme, and the

1993 edition explains how this operates at three levels. First, the company keeps its own house in order through activities such as an environmental audit. Secondly it takes environmental impact into account in its lending. Finally, it supports environmental groups which help to inform the public.

There are many routes to communicating with the public. Local liaison committees have served as a forum for local debate among pressure groups, industry and regulators for many years, and numerous successful examples exist. Public meetings also have a role, but should not be reserved for circumstances when there is a problem or complaint. It is clearly advantageous to provide a forum for regular 'liaison group' meetings to discuss issues of mutual concern and fill the void that often exists with the different parties only getting together under the adversarial conditions of a public inquiry or court. Open days or site visits, press announcements, and a whole range of educational links (school visits, information and activity packs, work experience for children, teacher secondment . . .) are other opportunities to raise the level of public awareness of your operations and environmental performance. Supermarkets are particularly prolific in supplying free literature on environmental issues.

Providing environmental information in an organization's annual report and accounts is another route for informing the public. Some organizations do this, although to varying extents. A survey reported in the *Financial Times* (15 January 1992) indicated that only 3 per cent of a sample of 670 annual reports highlighted environmental information in a separate statement. Most disclosures were quoted as being 'of such a low level to be virtually meaningless', but there is a growing pattern of providing more quantitative data, often in response to consultation with wide stakeholder groups. A more recent survey [7] of 100 companies in USA, Europe and Japan disclosed that 'duty to the environment' was a major reason for reporting, while public relations was second everywhere. Shareholder and pressure group influences were significant in USA and Japan, and constituted a major readership for 78 per cent of US companies, although 96 per cent regarded their own employees as the critical group. In Europe, competitive advantage was recognized by 18 per cent of companies surveyed, and 68 per cent identified business customers as the main target group for readership. The local community and environmental groups were also important to 70 per cent of US and 65 per cent of European companies.

Norsk Hydro in the UK was among the earliest to report its environmental performance in 1990, with verifying comments from Lloyd's Register. BP reported in 1991, while the first from British Gas and ICI were published in 1992. ICI's report to shareholders is noteworthy, admitting prosecutions and demonstrating an irrevocable commitment to objectives. It also included more detail than many others, and like the BP Chemicals newspaper dispelled the myth that much data on wastes could not be collected and could not be communicated to the non-specialist reader. The approach clearly demonstrates commitment to the public, but also raises commitment within the organization. Any response by managers to find reasons why something cannot be done gradually turns into commitment. External verification is needed, however, if environmental reporting is to be regarded as more than a mere public relations exercise. Enlightened business leaders recognize that a key reason for reporting is to secure a company's competitive position.

We must not forget that there are also the legal obligations of providing information in public registers. The registers of authorizations under the provisions of the Environmental Protection Act 1990 form an important example in the UK. Several environmental reports have been considerably more open about good and bad environmental performance than the law requires, as we have seen. The arguments about environmental issues have to be communicated to consumers, whose concerns are influenced by many factors. Technical arguments do not always hold up against the value judgements of the community.

Media relations are an important part of the communication process because this group has an influence on a broader audience as the public opinion surveys have indicated. Making information fully available to the media through regular briefings may strengthen rapport and encourage supportive articles. This may be a benefit when controversial issues arise, and contact should not be curtailed when negative issues emerge. Reporters may not have an opportunity to research thoroughly, and a simple presentation of controversial issues is often needed. The strategy of involvement may promote awareness of problems and so encourage fair and accurate representation.

The European Chemical Industry Federation (CEFIC) has produced proposals on external communications but they are not prescriptive, recognizing that various countries and regions differ in their culture, value systems, community infrastructure, response capabilities and regulatory requirements. Indeed, The UNEP report[3] points out that while environmental issues are of concern in developing countries, the more pressing nature of jobs and economic growth together with a lack of infrastructure are impediments to good communications. Public interest also seems greater when new building is taking place rather than relating to older plant. However, a number of common principles emerge.

Every organization should:

- Always adopt a positive attitude.
- Establish a policy on the voluntary communication of environmental information to the public, with adequate resources and arrangements being allocated to do so.
- Designate individual(s) to make contact with the public. The individual(s) should have environmental knowledge and communication skills.
- Handle all requests for information quickly and positively, and establish a continuous dialogue with local communities to better understand their

interests, anticipate their concerns, and provide information. The effectiveness of communication should be assessed in order to improve it.

- Look for opportunities to publicize good news and be aware of the need to reveal facts rapidly when problems occur.
- Provide the public with information to enable them to understand your activities. When possible tell them what you know—and what you do not. Acknowledge uncertainty, and if there is something you do not know, admit it. The information should be in a form which a non-specialist can understand.
- Consider the views of the public, local authorities, scientific organizations and other representative organizations when estimating the environmental impact of new developments.
- Keep your staff well informed. They are directly affected by your activities, but also serve as ambassadors to the community.
- Explain positively why certain information may need to be confidential. You may justify this on the grounds that releasing information may prejudice your competitiveness; endanger national or organization security; divulge confidential information from a third party or infringe an individual's privacy.
- Call in third parties: experts for advice and analysis, and be open with their findings.
- When information is requested that you do not have, consider carefully whether it is relevant and can reasonably be obtained.

Community perceptions of risk and community concerns are equally important as scientific factors, and should be remembered when making the public aware of environmental issues with the objective of persuading them that a proposed course of action is mutually desirable. Remember that:

1 Voluntary risks are accepted more readily than imposed risks.
2 People feel less concerned about risks over which they have control.
3 Risks that seem fair are accepted more than those that seem unfair.
4 Risk information from untrustworthy sources is less readily believed than from trustworthy sources.

So there are clear benefits in involving the community in the decision-making process at the earliest point and to the greatest extent possible. Late involvement conjures up visions of a cover-up. People are entitled to be involved in decisions affecting them, and involvement in the process leads to greater understanding and more appropriate reaction to risk. Some evidence suggests that citizens will less readily accept something they regard as risky if offered compensation than if given good information and a chance to participate in decision-making.[8] Offering them 'control' tends to increase responsibility and decreases opportunistic resistance, and can be achieved by inviting the public to join a local panel with power to inspect activities in the organization. A nuclear waste site in the USA has even given such a panel the ability to shut down its operations. Co-operation between the organization and the community by these routes can increase the organization's credibility and promote trust in its performance. It also creates a sound basis of understanding that will be of value if an accident should occur with potentially adverse environmental impact. Organizations need to plan not just for day to day issues, but also prepare for communications about a potential environmental incident.

Independent experts may make a useful contribution. While members of the community may learn enough to be well informed about a local issue, more detailed technical information may be difficult for them to understand. Regulatory and industrial experts may not appear impartial, and independent consultants have a role here, but should not be introduced at the adversarial stage of an issue. Involve external expertise early. Funding by business of independent experts hired by community groups may be appropriate. There is also a provision in the Superfund Amendments and Reauthorization Act in the USA for funding to support independent technical advice on amelioration measures. Of course, the expert must be able to communicate well with the community, and not feel more at ease with the technical personnel from the regulators or companies involved.

Another communication principle is to release information early, for these reasons:

- People are entitled to information that affects, or they perceive affects, their lives.
- Delay may allow information to leak, resulting in lost trust and credibility.
- Prompt release of information is more likely to lead to meaningful involvement in decision-making.
- Those first releasing information have better control over its accuracy.
- People tend to overestimate risks if information is withheld.

Address community concerns when explaining risk and answer the often silent question 'what does it mean to me?'. Put information in an appropriate context and perspective by choosing risk comparisons carefully. Taking examples of some more alarming and some reassuring comparisons than the risk of concern allows fair understanding of a situation.

Effective communication must be supported actively and visibly at all levels of management, and remember that the community decides what is acceptable to it. As a result, bad news on environmental performance from outside the organization must effectively be directed to those who can act upon it and not be resisted by barriers that are automatically raised. It is therefore important that a communication infrastructure must exist within the organization to motivate and facilitate learning about environmental issues. Recognizing this as an opportunity for improving the environmental performance of an organization is a message from the following case history.

Case Study: Sybron Chemicals Inc. winner of the Public Relations Society of America Silver Anvil Award, 1990 for the best community relations programme in the USA[9]

Public pressure to close down this small speciality chemical manufacturer after several environmental incidents forced the company to realize that its survival depended on it becoming a 'caring neighbour' rather than 'keeping things at arm's length'. Two-way communication was an inherent feature of this culture change which included installing a sophisticated telecommunication system for contacting neighbours in the event of an incident. It also operates in an inquiry mode by playing recorded information on the plant status, while callers seeking further information can leave a message on an answering service. This system also serves as an alert system, advising operators of problems. The company also responded to views from community perception surveys by introducing a quarterly newsletter, plant tours and open house events, and monthly meetings of a Neighbourhood Involvement Committee. Volunteers from the community were also trained to identify odours in order that they can report accurate information to the company. This two-way communication programme is thus an integral part of the company's environmental performance and not merely a mouthpiece for it.

Communicating Within

At the most obvious level, one has only to look back at almost any major pollution incident to appreciate the role of people in causing environmental harm, or conversely in maintaining good environmental performance.

'It's all down to people and attitudes.'

Environmental Manager, Rover Group

Communication within the organization is the key to maintaining good environmental performance and reducing the risk of problems in the future. Selection of the right people, training them to do the right things, and motivating them to maintain performance are critical factors. An organization's staff are some of its greatest ambassadors for communication to the public, but equally will betray poor performance.

There is also an increasing legal responsibility to provide environmental education and training. Take for example the BATNEEC concept discussed in Chapter 4. As we have explained the T stands for 'techniques' and not merely 'technology' as used in early European air pollution legislation. The concept of 'techniques' embraces both the process and how it is operated. In practice it is taken to mean the concept and design of the process, the components of which it is composed and the manner in which they are connected. It also includes matters such as numbers and qualifications of staff, working methods, training and supervision, and the design, construction, layout and maintenance of buildings. This imperative is not surprising. Despite technological advances improving the environmental integrity and reliability of equipment and plant, people continue to play a critical role in the design, operation, maintenance and management of systems, and also in their failures. Modelling human performance and quantifying probabilities of human error are complex procedures requiring specialist skills, and as such are outside the scope of this book.

Case study: United Technologies Corporation[10]

'There have been violations in the past. They haven't set in motion a process to make sure there is continual compliance. So we have to assume that they have not taken their corporate environmental responsibilities very seriously.'

This was the assessment of an Environmental Protection Agency administrator on United Technologies which, despite integrating its corporate environmental and health and safety staff under one Director of Human and Natural Resource Protection, had failed to produce a consistent approach across the company.

Such severe criticism together with the fines for non-compliance spurred the company to pay more attention to environmental issues. In 1989, a new corporate policy was developed and disseminated to all employees to demonstrate that environmental issues would be treated as core business issues. Environmental standards were revised and environmental training provided, not only for professionals, but also for managers and the workforce, who are often directly involved in the handling and disposal of potential pollutants. So far so good, but the organizational structure did not reflect the importance of environmental issues, because the functional responsibility stopped two levels away from the chief executive. A new appointment at senior vice-president level, with direct access to the chief executive dealt with this problem, but there was still a question of linking corporate and operating unit staff. Environmental executive posts at each operating unit with direct line reporting to the senior vice-president as well as the business unit heads provided the missing link. Collectively these executives formed an Environmental Council, meeting monthly to set corporate policies, standards and strategies, while day-to-day environmental programmes were dealt with at each operating unit level. Five key elements of the expanding environmental programme were announced in 1991. They were:

- Training: to raise environmental awareness among all managers, provide compliance regulations for relevant staff and address attitudes to environmental issues.
- Audit all operations regularly.
- Develop environmental data management systems to monitor environmental performance, give early warning of trends or potential problems, and to aid regulatory reporting requirements.
- Examine materials, processes and techniques to improve the design, manufacture and use of the company's products, and thereby reduce waste and pollution.
- Participate in the development of legislation and regulatory measures likely to affect company activities.

Implicit in this example is the integration of communication in the environmental management system of an organization. Before moving on let us examine some aspects of this management system in more detail.

Develop a coherent management system

We have previously drawn on the parallels between energy and environmental management. The evolution of an environmental management programme, depicted in Table 7.1, can be developed from one for energy.[11] This scheme provides an instrument for analysing how an organization's programme is developing.

It should be evident that policy, structure and reporting systems need to evolve in parallel for effectiveness, and are integral parts of the management system. The purpose of environmental reporting is to provide management information, which is useless if there is no management structure to make use of it. Similarly, a management structure without a policy framework will be ineffective. Clearly, this is an idealistic situation, and policies will rarely develop before staffing, structures and responsibilities are established. Progress along several fronts is likely, but the Scheme of Table 7.1 serves to keep the overall programme in balance. Any column that leaves the state of development of the others significantly behind is likely to result in lack of purpose and effectiveness. So, for example, an organization with a top management policy (level 1), an established structure (level 4) and a reporting system to level 2 would result in site personnel having limited data but no reporting structure to match. Motivation will surely fail under such circumstances.

Growing numbers of organizations are addressing these issues. An ardent exponent of environmental auditing is Union Carbide. With a reputation scarred by the Bhopal disaster, improvement in management has included a corporate requirement for environmental policy since 1987. Ownership of day-

Table 7.1   Levels of development of an environmental management programme

Policy	Structure	Reporting system
0 No explicit policy.	No explicit structure.	Emphasis on costs.
1 Top management declare an active commitment to environmental issues.	An Environment Committee is established at site or plant level.	Monthly reports of environmental performance possibly based on intermittent measurements.
2 Environmental issues are explicitly the responsibility of a technical manager.	Staff at site level are designated with part-time responsibility for environmental issues.	Aggregate measurements of environmental performance.
3 Top management recognize the potential of environmental management, and exhort middle managers to give attention to environmental issues.	Responsibility for environmental issues at site level is allocated to an individual.	Quantification is based on measurement at sub-unit level.
4 Target system introduced to direct middle managers to environmental issues.	Creation of environmental management structure involving top and operational management and incorporating designations such as 'environmental supervisor' in workforce.	Accountability at sub-unit level based on measurements of appropriate variables.

to-day environmental management is delegated to plant managers, who may spend half their time on health, safety and environmental issues. Their pay is linked to achieving environmental objectives, which are monitored by a vice-president reporting directly to the chairman. An example in Chapter 8 Section 7 illustrates some conflicts in organizations which have failed to address the issues effectively.

Raise staff awareness

Much has been written about the efficient use of human resources in organizations, and we can combine the necessary attributes along three dimensions: capability, alignment and motivation. Progress along the first dimension requires giving staff the knowledge, skills and attitudes to work efficiently and effectively, but they also need resources. It is relatively easy to oversupply in this dimension. Appointing overqualified staff, sending people on courses and providing expensive facilities create a good image, but may achieve little without movement along the other dimensions. Progress along these other dimensions may be more difficult.

On alignment, all staff need to know your organization's environmental policies, objectives and routes to achieving these. Staff need to know their role and

Table 7.2   Possible causes of staff failure to implement good environmental practice

	System	Individual
Alignment	*Information* Staff do not know how well to perform Misleading performance information No performance feedback	*Ability* Poor staff selection Poor job match
Capability	*Resources* Insufficient materials Insufficient equipment Insufficient people Inadequate organization	*Skills and knowledge* Inadequate environmental education or training
Motivation	*Incentives and rewards* Little use of non-monetary incentives Good performance not rewarded No differentiation in rewards	*Attitudes* Lack of interest Fear of failure

to be dedicated to it through leadership. This dedication is commitment and has to be earned; it cannot be imposed. Commitment is also associated with the third dimension: motivation. Staff must trust management and feel that this trust is reciprocated to ensure motivation. The three-dimensional concepts can be expanded into a matrix (Table 7.2)

Poor environmental performance may result from a deficit in any of the six segments of this matrix. In this section we explore many of the aspects of improving human performance in an environmental management system.

Provide leadership

Environmental awareness needs to be created in appropriate detail at the different levels within an organization. The numbers of personnel clearly differ in the various levels (Figure 7.3), as does the type of information needed by the

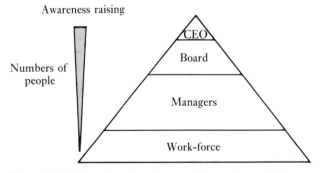

Figure 7.3   Expansion of numbers needing environmental awareness

individuals concerned according to their job function. However, the most powerful model that employees have is their own boss, so management and supervisory levels are key links in disseminating the message.

The pinnacle is occupied by business leaders, and leadership is the starting point for good environmental performance, but how do you get top management support? A starting point must be raising awareness of the driving forces summarized in Chapter 2. The legal pressures, market forces, public pressures, shareholder demands and other constraints make it difficult for business leaders to ignore environmental issues, but they should not be regarded as a separate consideration. Top level commitment is achieved when the chief executive officer appreciates the environmental problems in the organization and resolves to deal with them. The hallmark of executives is 'doing', and commitment involves more than merely stating an intention to deal with environmental protection. Concern for the environment must be as important as concern for profits, and true leadership is essential to demonstrate this. The chief executive of Union Carbide spends one-third of his time on public affairs activities, and environmental matters form a large part of that third. He has suggested that it is the power of senior management to create discontent: discontent with the status quo. Cast aside the comfort and familiarity of old policies and procedures, and 'the way we've always done it'.[12] That response should always raise the alarm bells and signal that resources are being used inefficiently with the potential of causing environmental pollution.

One instrument for demonstrating commitment is to state and publicize a goal. The goal should be a simple statement of where you want the organization to be. It should state quite simply that the organization will conduct its activities responsibly and in a manner that will protect from harm its staff, the public and the environment. The BP Environmental Policy Statement discussed in Chapter 3 is a good example. From the goal emerges a plan. Most activities of an organization have the potential to harm people or the environment. The plan establishes mandatory corporate standards in the form of policies and procedures. The example in the next chapter on elimination of ozone depleting chemicals highlights such a plan.

A positive signal that commitment has been secured is to allocate adequate resources in terms of finance, facilities and staff. The costs should not be underestimated. Large organizations spend large sums, but small organizations can demonstrate similar commitment and benefit from returns that can have short payback. Remember, 'Pollution Prevention Pays' and examples of this occur throughout this book.

Environmental considerations are just part of the overall management issues to be taken into account in any decison, and as such are on a par with quality, finance and so on.Unfortunately managers do not always treat them so. In this regard it is worth noting a comment in the *British Gas Environmental Review*, 1991.[13] Independent pilot audits revealed among other things:

'The need for more guidance to be given to managers on the interpretation and application of the company's environmental policy.'

This clearly pointed to the need for more appropriate management guidelines, information and training.

British Rail's *Green Book* has been issued to about 1500 senior managers to inform them about principal environmental effects, legislation and regulatory requirements. Possible technical or management solutions for improved performance are offered together with a contact route to an internal consultant for advice. Another example is the Code of Professional Practice on 'Engineers and the Environment' adopted by the Engineering Council in the UK from 1 March 1994, and supported by *Guidelines on Environmental Issues* published later in 1994. More generally, a Code of Environmental Ethics for Engineers has been drafted by the World Federation of Engineering Organizations and approved by the European Federation of National Engineering Associations and the United Nations Education Scientific and Cultural Organization.[14]

The incentives introduced by positive objectives such as those of ICI also serve to motivate managers (Table 7.3). Wide publication of the objectives resulted in them being integrated into the corporate philosophy. Managers are then responsible for ensuring that the objectives are met, and achieving this includes identifying, training and motivating staff.

Table 7.3 ICI Group Environmental Objectives announced in 1991

All new plants to be built to the most demanding standards: this will normally require the use of the best environmental practice

Wastes to be reduced by 50% by 1995, and an attempt to be made to eliminate off-site disposal of environmentally harmful wastes

High priority to energy and resource conservation, with emphasis on reducing environmental effects

Recycling policies to be established within the group and with customers

Attitudes to the Environment

Just as in communicating to the public, the different attitudes and perceptions of people within the organization must be addressed, and it is useful to identify attitudes to environmental issues. The square shown in Figure 7.4 provides an instrument for looking at the attitudes of individuals. The idea is to mark in the square the position that represents your attitude. Where will you place your cross? Change 'environmental protection' for 'energy efficiency', 'sustainable development' or whatever is your current concern. Invariably some people place their tick towards the bottom with one or two on the bottom left. Clearly the aim is for everyone to tick the top right hand corner. We all have a part to play in using energy efficiently, in avoiding waste and in helping to protect the

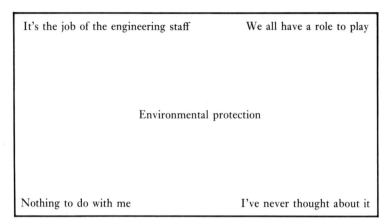

Figure 7.4   What is your position on environmental issues?

environment. It has been said that environmental protection is the 'integral of individual human actions', and we have to achieve this by the total involvement of staff. They need to be made aware of their roles and responsibilities through leadership, training and motivation.

Organizations are made up of individuals with a variety of personality types which are continuously interacting and these interactions are likely to have effects on the performance of an organization. Leadership needs to recognize these interactions and to understand how they may be used to improve the performance of the organization. A concept linking the organization, its culture and the individuals provides a framework for assessing the organization and how it interacts with environmental problems. The objective is motivated staff who accept and believe in the importance of environmental management in a similar manner to commitment to quality management. The four attitude types from Figure 7.4 can be developed further to produce Table 7.4, which includes some job titles often found to relate to the attitude roles.

The key elements of any organization are the individuals, and motivation of individuals is essential. Just as organizations have objectives, so do individuals.

Table 7.4   What attitudes to environmental issues exist in your organizational structure?

Who are the influencers?	Environment manager; general manager; union representatives; sales and marketing; customers; health and safety personnel.
Who are the blockers?	Financial managers; project engineers; shop-floor personnel.
Who are the workers?	Environment manager; health and safety personnel; site services personnel; conservationists.
Who don't know?	General manager; directors; shop-floor personnel; financial managers.
Who don't care?	Shop-floor personnel; suppliers; personnel department.

Motivation is the key to sustaining momentum for improved environmental performance; leadership helps people climb the levels of commitment by raising this motivation (Figure 7.5).

In all cases, it is essential to introduce a complete environmental management system with totally supportive and interacting components, as we illustrated previously in this chapter. Speaking recently, an environmental manager from a large UK business related that an environmental awareness pack for staff had been introduced too soon; the supporting environmental management system was not in place.

Twiss and Goodridge[15] identified the characteristics of organizations having an external orientation, a focus on user needs and receptivity to user ideas. Such 'learning organizations' accept that everyone has a contribution to make, but this is only possible within an open culture in which communication is possible in all directions. Communication alone is not sufficient, however, for there must be a readiness to accept proposals from all levels within an organization. Such an 'open' culture reflects the view that a person doing a job often knows best and can identify improvements if they are motivated so to do.

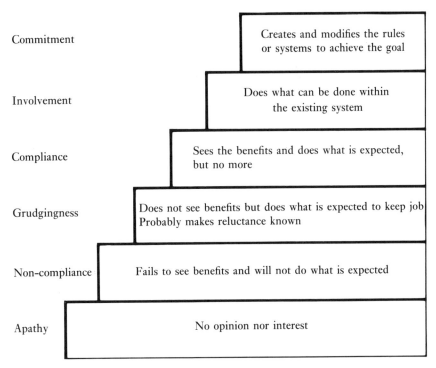

Figure 7.5   The steps to commitment

Another analysis of organizational structure and culture theories[16] suggested that the most common structure for medium to large firms is the machine bureaucracy/professional bureaucracy. The machine-type is common because many activities include routine, repetitive work, with the result that the co-ordinating mechanism is standardization of work processes. Formal communication tends to be preferred, and the system responds slowly to attempts to introduce change towards environmental care. While a clear environmental policy supported with appropriate rules is likely to be followed, difficulties arise in circumstances where there are no rules and responses to unforeseen events may be inappropriate.

'Environmental awareness' has been a recurring theme throughout this chapter. The ICI Environmental Awareness Programme illustrates the role. The programme is directed at non-managerial staff and has the objectives of:

- Giving staff the capability to discuss the organization's projects and achievements with the general public.
- Enabling them to evaluate environmental issues in a balanced way.
- Letting them understand their role in environmental management.

Many organizations have recognized the role of staff awareness and training in improving environmental performance, and discharge the function in different ways. British Rail, for example, have given all staff a copy of the company environmental policy statement, and they are encouraged through the staff suggestion scheme to make proposals for improvements. Quality Improvement Teams to tackle environmental issues have also been formed. Training is also being developed through distance learning and through a telephone help service. Other organizations have such documentation, but do not distribute it widely to avoid management overload with information on environmental issues, health and safety, quality issues and so on. In fact a major engineering group is integrating these manuals into a single information source with the option of electronic access making the information more readily accessible.

Communication is a key feature of an integrated environmental management programme, but ultimately the issue turns to behavioural problems, with organizations building environmental values, standards and practice into the heart of the corporate culture.

Ownership is an essential ingredient of managing an organization to improve environmental quality. Ownership assigns responsibility for design, operation and improvement of processes and activities. Emerging systems of environmental quality management in Europe aim to give ownership of environmental responsibility to organizations. Such integration of environmental management systems into the daily operations of an organization is a key feature of the self-regulation policy in the Netherlands as outlined in Chapter 2, for example, and increasingly so in the UK.

Quotations from conversations with environmental managers in two large organizations demonstrate the growing realization of this approach

'We're encouraging people to take responsibility and to be responsible.'

Environmental Manager, Rover Power Train, Rover Group (May 1992)

'All the rest of what we're trying to do is a waste of time unless we get the people on board.'

Group Environmental Technology Manager, ICI (May 1992)

Human factors play a major role in many major environmental problems as the Bhopal incident demonstrated. It has been suggested that while established techniques could have identified the engineering aspects of the problem, they may not have prevented the incident. Indeed, applying such techniques can be a waste of time if basic safety requirements (the 'hard' aspects such as technical features) are ignored through the 'soft' problem areas involving people, as was apparently true in this case.[17]

The organizational, personal and technical perspectives are not independent, but interact. However, even integrating them does not prevent problems, for we often find:

- Overconfidence in technology.
- Failure to recognize interactions among system components which have been designed relatively independently.
- Failure to recognize people problems.
- Failure to anticipate the combination of unlikely events.

An approach used by some organizations to build up the human resource base, to keep up to date on environmental developments and to tap external expertise is to establish environmental advisory boards. Several national and multinational organizations have advisory boards comprising members drawn from different countries and meeting three or four times each year. The boards serve to introduce external viewpoints into environmental decision-making and recognize that a view from within may not see the wider picture.

A board may emanate from a company's environmental policy and combine with a formal quality assurance scheme to monitor environmental performance, or allow an organization to test policies against external views. A variation of the external environmental advisory board is used by certain financial institutions to screen 'environmental' investment portfolios. The effectiveness of an advisory board depends on the independence of members and the willingness of the organization to participate in discussion at the appropriate time. Acting on advice is an important motivator to the advisory board, as is the provision of adequate resources.

As the organization usually selects members, sets the agenda, supplies information and serves as the secretariat, it is clearly easy for it to obstruct the work of the group and make it ineffective. Strategic issues may have commercial sensitivity which may preclude involvement of a board in discussion at an early stage, but an external view on main board decisions can be useful. Environmental advisory boards also have a public relations benefit, but this may backfire if disagreements lead to resignations.

Conclusion

Environmental problems are 'soft' systems problems and involve interactions of people with 'hard' technology. Engineering solutions are important and have been covered earlier, but alone they are unlikely to succeed.

Communication within the organization is the key to maintaining good environmental performance. Selection of the right people, training them to do the right things, and motivating them to maintain performance are critical factors. An organization's staff are some of its greatest ambassadors for communication to the public but, equally, they will betray poor performance.

Organizations operate in society and must be acceptable to society. Unacceptability may be attributed in some circumstances to the failure of the public to appreciate environmental risks in relation to other risks. Communication is a key to securing public confidence in an enterprise so that it may be strong enough to withstand the doubts that arise when problems occur.

Practical Points for Action

- Have you identified your key processes?
- Have you assigned ownership of each key process to an individual?
- Do the owners recognize their responsibility for maintaining, operating and improving their process?
- Always adopt a positive attitude to environmental information: recognize the opportunities for voluntary communication of environmental information to the public, with adequate resources and arrangements being allocated to do so.
- Establish a dialogue with local communities to better understand their interests, anticipate their concerns, and provide information.
- Look for opportunities to publicize good news and be aware of the need to reveal facts rapidly when problems occur.
- Ensure that information is in a form which a non-specialist can understand.
- Consider the views and attitudes of others when communicating about environmental issues.
- Keep your staff well informed. They are directly affected by your activities, have a direct impact on your environmental performance, and also serve as ambassadors to the community.
- Question carefully whether any information has to be confidential.

● Consider using 'outsiders' for impartial advice and analysis, and to assist in communication to the community.

References

1 Department of the Environment, *The UK Environment*, HMSO, London, 1992.
2 M. Seymour, 'Crafting a Crisis Communications Plan', *Directors & Boards*, vol. 15, no. 4, 1991, 26–29.
3 'Companies' Organisation and Public Communication on Environmental Issues', UNEP/IEO, Paris, 1991, Foreword.
4 R. E. Kasperson, O. Renn, P. Slovic, H. S. Brown, J. Emel, R. Gobb, J. X. Kasperson, and S. Ratick, 'The Social Amplification of Risk: A Conceptual Framework', *Risk Analysis*, vol. 8, 1988, 177–187.
5 A. Fisher, 'Risk Communication Challenges', *Risk Analysis*, vol. 11, 1991, 173–179.
6 UNEP/IEO, 'Companies' Organisation and Public Communication on Environmental Issues', UNEP/IEO, Paris, 1991, 22.
7 ENDS Report 218 March 1993, p. 3 Reference to survey by Deloitte Touche Tohmatsu International.
8 S. G. Hadden, 'Public Perception of Hazardous Waste', *Risk Analysis*, vol. 11, 1991, 47–57.
9 'The Organisational Links Between Risk Communication and Risk Management: the Case of Sybron Chemicals Inc.', *Risk Analysis*, vol. 12, 1992, 431–438.
10 Adapted from *Directors & Boards*, vol. 15, no. 4, 1991, 14–16.
11 Armitage Norton Report, *Energy Conservation Investment in Industry, An Appraisal of the Barriers*, Energy paper no. 50, HMSO, London, 1982.
12 R. Kennedy, 'Keynote Address', 2nd World Industrial Conference on Environmental Management, Rotterdam, April, 1991, International Chamber of Commerce.
13 British Gas, *British Gas Environmental Review*, 1991, Corporate Affairs Directorate, London, November, 1991.
14 The Engineering Council, 10 Maltravers Street, London, WC2 3ER.
15 O. O. Twiss and M. Goodridge, *Management Technology for Competitive Advantage*, Pitman, London, 1989.
16 J. A. Huggard, C. P. George, and A.-M. Warris, 'The Continuous Development of an Environmental Assurance (Audit) Manual and Guidance System Based on Plant Experience & Organisational Theory', *Environmental Pollution 1*, *ICEP-1*, *Proceedings*, vol. 1, Inderscience, Geneva, 1991, 71–81.
17 T. A. Kletz, 'Eliminating Potential Process Hazards', *Chemical Engineering*, 1 April 1985, 48–61.

8

Practical Examples of Integrated Environmental Management

In this chapter we give some real examples from several countries of many of the principles we have developed throughout the book. While some are clearly identified with a particular organization, others are simply designated as relating to anonymous organizations, but nevertheless reflect true situations.

1   Threats and Opportunities in Leather Making

One stage in the making of leather from sheepskin pelts involves degreasing. For many years to 1991, Eastern Counties Leather of Cambridgeshire UK carried out the process with tetrachloroethane, a commonly used dry cleaning and degreasing solvent. In August 1983, tests for organochlorine compounds in the water supply to St Ives, Cambridgeshire, revealed higher than expected levels, which were traced to contamination at a borehole near the leather company. In October 1983, the water company closed the water pumping station fed by the borehole. Three years later, the water company started legal action to recover costs for damages in respect of sinking a new borehole and installing new pumping equipment. The company's case was based on contamination of the aquifer by spillages of the chemical over a 20-year period from the site of Eastern Counties Leather. As a result, the water company could no longer draw water from the aquifer. On the grounds of the common law tort set down in the case of Rylands *vs* Fletcher of 1868, there is the principle of strict liability that the polluter should pay, but a subsequent House of Lords ruling held that this only applied if an escape of pollutant was caused by non-natural activities. Consequently in 1991, the legal judgment accepted that there had been spillages over the years, but that these were inevitable in the nature of the defendant's activities. In carrying out natural operations, the issue was considered 'the natural and anticipated consequences of an escape', and as the contamination had not occurred through 'non-natural' activities, the polluter could not be held responsible for the costs of clean-up or compensation. On appeal in November 1992, this judgment was overturned on the basis of the Ballard *vs* Tomlinson case of 1885, which stipulated anyone abstracting water from an underground source is entitled to do so in its natural state. Hence the court decided liability on the basis that it related to natural rights incidental to the ownership of land. Nuisance had been proven and so strict liability should apply. The Appeal Court ruled that the polluter should pay compensation amounting to £1.7 million: an example of the polluter pays principle. Further implications were the possibility of action under the Water Resources Act for the costs of remediation of the aquifer, as well as regulatory prosecution for polluting the aquifer.

In December 1993, the House of Lords judged that the prerequisite of liability under the Rylands *vs* Fletcher case was that the damage from the escape of a dangerous substance should be foreseeable. As those responsible at the leather company could not at the appropriate time have foreseen that damage to the aquifer might occur, the payment of damages was over-ruled. In giving the judgment, the Lords added that it was more appropriate for strict liability for operations of high risk to be imposed by statute rather than by case law, in order that operators of such activities could be clear about their obliga-tions. The wider implications of this case relating to insurer liability to cover retrospective pollution under old policies had been closely watched by in-surance companies. The undermining of the polluter pays principle will lead to detailed consideration of the issue by legislators, and comparisons will in-evitably be drawn with the strict liability applied elsewhere. Ironically, the leather company had won an award for responsible environmental manage-ment, indicating that current good practice may not prevent anxieties from past events.

On the positive side it is possible to cite examples of waste minimization, and Eastern Counties Leather now uses a solvent-free degreasing process. Other pollution problems can come from trace metals used in the process. In particular, there have been growing pressures in many countries to reduce dis-charges of chromium, the traditional tanning agent for leather. Tanning is the chemical process by which putrescible animal hides are rendered stable, and a common agent for this is trivalent chromium in acidic conditions. Statutory limits on releases of this metal to the environment make treatment by end-of-pipe techniques increasingly expensive.

In the past up to 40 per cent of the chromium compounds used in the tanning of leather may be discharged in the waste water flow, thereby representing a loss of resource as well as a potential risk of causing harm to the environment. Con-ventional end-of-pipe treatments involving precipitation of chromium com-pounds as a sludge may address the water pollution problem, but in so doing they produce a solid waste for disposal, and there are increasing constraints on the disposal of sludges. The attendant risk of land pollution and long-term threat of leachate migrating to underground water clearly raises questions of whether the end-of-pipe approach is the best practicable environmental option. A cleaner technology approach pioneered in the Germanakos tannery at Piraeus near Athens illustrates both the technical approach to recycling and routes for disseminating information. The UNEP Cleaner Production Programme was established by the Industry and Environment Programme Activity Centre in May 1989. Publications such as *Cleaner Production Worldwide*[1] from the UNEP programme illustrate the variety of approaches to preventing pollution at source through cost-effective solutions. Industry sector working groups aim to build databases of cleaner production processes and to expand the awareness of cleaner production through networking to exchange and update information. The Athens case study is an example summarized in the UNEP report and also promoted through the Tanning Network.[2] The project itself resulted from collaboration between the Greek and Dutch governments.

In the Athens plant, hides are tanned with basic chromium sulphate, and after treatment the solution flows from the tanning drums along gutters to a collection pit via a sieve to remove fibres. Positioning the removable gutters under the drum outlet valves must be done carefully to avoid spillage. From the collection pit the liquor is pumped to a treatment tank to which a calculated amount of magnesium oxide is added and the solution made alkaline. Stirring the mixture for over two hours results in the production of chromium hydroxide, which is allowed to settle as a sludge and after separation from the liquid is dissolved in a calculated amount of sulphuric acid. The product is basic chromium sulphate, which is recycled as the starting material for the process. The recovery efficiency is 95–98 per cent while a 99.9 per cent reduction in chromium in the effluent is achieved. Payback to the tannery was achieved in 11 months, and the product quality was more consistent.

Finally we can consider an example of the preferred option in pollution prevention heirarchy, that of material change to avoid generating the pollutant in the first instance. ICI and Tioxide developed an alternative to chromium-based tanning agents in a product comprising a complex of aluminium, titanium and magnesium salts. This alternative tanning agent may be used with traditional equipment, but also offers other benefits in addition to the reduced pollution loads. These benefits include reduced water and chemical consumption, and shorter processing times, yielding a product which may be dyed more easily than that from the traditional route. Once again, there is a demonstration that pollution prevention can yield additional benefits which may be particularly crucial to the business performance of small and medium sized enterprises, and do not compromise product quality. The choice between the options in the hierarchy will depend on the choice of particular organizations. One with modern, cost-effective plant may prefer to continue with well-tried production processes and add new plant for recycling and regeneration, while another, who may in any case wish to upgrade plant, could incorporate means of utilizing environmentally beneficial, alternative chemicals. The implications for skilled operation will also enter the equation that each company must solve for itself, in the light of prevailing circumstances.

2 Integrated Environmental Management in a Mineral Water Bottling Plant

A major problem facing many organizations is the growing pressure to deal with packaging wastes of various types. Waste minimization and recycling are key factors in any approach to sustainable development, and both have to be taken together to avoid the main criticisms of the German packaging law, that has been so successful in collecting recycled materials that there are insufficient national outlets for the collected materials. We have referred to these problems in previous chapters. Other countries have also introduced measures to manage packaging waste, and these include France, Belgium and Austria.

In Austria, the Federal Waste Management Plan includes among its aims the promotion of waste minimization. Producers have responsibility for the packaging of their products, and every member of a distribution chain is required to take back all waste packaging from its products, or to participate in existing collection and recycling systems. Included in the Waste Management Plan is the requirement that beverage containers are reused or recycled at specified levels by the year 2000. For bottled water packaging the target rate is 96 per cent. In fact water provides a classic illustration of a reusable resource, with circulation through the water cycle. A mineral water bottling plant in Austria embraces the principle of reuse together with recycling of packaging and other materials to provide a model demonstration of waste minimization principles.

Tritium and carbon-14 dating show that the water drawn from underground and bottled at Romerquelle Gesellschaft mbH fell some 5000 years before re-emergence from the wells. The company takes the view that the water quality has not changed since antiquity, and the quality of future resources should be preserved. An environmental policy is written into the company guidelines, and a survey by market researchers revealed concern for the environment and quality of the water resource prevalent throughout the staff at all levels. While management provide leadership, they also maintain that positive attitudes to the environment must be developed from below, and cannot simply be imposed from above.

From the following outline it will become clear that the company aims to have a completely closed system, to conserve and protect environmental resources, and as a by-product to yield economic benefits through reuse and recycling.

The water supply comes from five boreholes some 300 m distant from the factory buildings. The water emerges under its own pressure and is is totally enclosed in stainless steel throughout its passage along pipework to storage tanks and thence to the bottling plant. The temperature of the water is 16 °C as it leaves the ground, and this provides some space-heating in part of the buildings.

A refundable deposit system (4 Austrian schillings) ensures that 99.5 per cent of the glass bottles in which the water is packaged are recycled. The bottles themselves have to be washed to ensure bacteriological quality. Phosphates and other substances difficult to treat in effluents are avoided, and the desired quality is best achieved with an alkaline (sodium hydroxide) solution. The resulting alkaline waste cannot pass directly to an effluent treatment plant, but is neutralized by contact with the acidic gases from the main heating plant, which is fuelled by oil containing sulphur. The acidic sulphur dioxide produced during combustion neutralizes the alkaline aqueous waste, rendering both to an acceptable pH value. The combustion products are then discharged from a chimney, while the aqueous waste passes to a water treatment plant. This plant includes biological treatment in a rotating biological contactor and treatment with aluminium hydroxide, which is obtained by recycling the aluminium from bottle cap covers. Strict discharge limits are enforced by the local water pollution inspectorate, and samples of the final treated water are taken daily and passed to the inspectorate for test. In a past incident, cadmium contamination of the effluent breached the permitted discharge limits. It was soon found, however, that the metal was a contaminant in the 'imported' microorganisms used for the biological treatment plant. This problem demonstrates the potential influence of raw materials on environmental impact, and the need for monitoring quality throughout the supply chain. The final effluent from the factory is of sufficiently high quality to discharge to the local River Wiesgrabenbach, with no detriment to the water quality. Sludge from the biological treatment plant is provided free of charge to the local farmers to avoid them being tempted to use artificial fertilizers with consequent risk of future contamination of the local environment and ultimately the future water resource. The land surrounding the factory is also owned by the company as a further attempt to protect the water from pollution.

Further examples of recycling are the conversion of plastic from the bottle caps to bottle cases, while the paper from bottle labels also goes for recycling. The bottle labels themselves are affixed with casein glue rather than synthetic alternatives as another demonstration of integrating environmental concern through the use of natural products.

Benefits

Energy recycling has been introduced to reduce primary energy consumption by 40 per cent (with the consultants being paid directly from the savings realized—a useful incentive for success!). The latest offices and buildings for a new bottling line are being built with ecological considerations in mind in terms of features such as insulation. In the longer term, the company aims to be self-sufficient in heat and electricity. The total recycling benefits to the company materialized as a profit of 5 million Austrian schillings in 1990, and the financial base of the company is demonstrated by all developments being funded from capital without borrowing.

3 Reacting to the Phase Out of Ozone Depleting Substances

The development of chlorofluorocarbons (CFCs) was hailed as a great achievement. The compounds had been designed for their low toxicity and high chemical stability, and found wide use as aerosol propellants, refrigerants, plastic foam expansion agents and industrial solvents in the electronics industry. In 1974, the first suggestions appeared that CFCs were a potential source of chlorine in the upper atmosphere (stratosphere). This chlorine could result in reduction of the ozone concentrations in the stratosphere. The ozone acts as a shield protecting the surface of the earth from solar radiation in the ultraviolet region. Several key biomolecules, including DNA, absorb and are damaged by such ultraviolet radiation. Ozone provides an effective shield in this region, and its depletion in the stratosphere may have a deleterious effect on humans, on plants or on food chains.

As a result of these concerns, pressure mounted in the USA for reductions in the use of CFCs, especially in aerosol sprays, and by 1978 their use in many sprays was banned. Nevertheless concentrations of CFCs in the atmosphere continued to grow as a result of their many other uses. Reports suggest that for several years, monitoring from satellites had indicated a large drop of some 40 per cent in total ozone over the Antarctic region during the southern spring, but NASA computers had been programmed to reject differences greater than ± 30 per cent, which may have resulted from instrumental drift or natural variability. It was not until Farman and his colleagues of the British Antarctic Survey, reported the difference in 1985 in a letter to the journal *Nature*, that the unexpected effect of a reduction was confirmed. (An important lesson to be learned here! Don't ignore measurements simply because they are unexpected.)

Continuing concern eventually led to the Montreal Protocol. In 1987 in Montreal, a conference supported by most of the CFC-using countries agreed a protocol for a 50 per cent reduction in CFC use by the year 2000. Continuing studies showed that such reductions would still result in doubling the amount of chlorine in the stratosphere by that date, and so a further conference was held in 1990. It was agreed that use of CFCs and other ozone depleting chemicals would be cut by 50 per cent by 1995, 85 per cent by 1997 and completely phased out by 2000. Some countries have agreed an earlier phase out.

In this example we explore a response to the external pressures for the phase out of stratospheric ozone depleting substances (ODS).

A worldwide company in the manufacture of communication equipment that is one of the major UK manufacturers of printed circuit boards for military and civil applications has been under increasing commercial pressures resulting from the environmental problems of ozone depletion in the upper atmosphere. The 1987 Montreal Protocol and US Clean Air legislation calling for reductions in the use of ozone depleting chemicals demanded a serious commitment from the company.

In 1989 the company estimated that at its 14 factory locations it was consuming at least 20 000 litres of chlorofluorocarbons (CFCs), mainly as solvents for cleaning the boards, together with other ODSs like trichloroethane. The CFC consumption alone represented about 0.75 per cent of the total UK use at the time. Senior management recognized that legislation was likely to lead to reductions in consumption, and that major customers, including the military would soon be seeking 'green' suppliers. The company consequently moved forward on a programme aimed at completely phasing out the use of CFCs by the end of 1993. This case history illustrates many of the features addressed in earlier chapters relating to waste and pollution elimination, in particular the use of an initial audit, staff awareness and support, clear timetabled targets, short- and long-term objectives, financial provision, research and investigation, training and eventual implementation within cost and timetable objectives.

The first stage was to undertake an audit of CFC consumption. This identified a wide range of products from several suppliers for degreasing and defluxing solders, for de-watering after plating and in ceramic and microwave production processes. Some CFCs were also being used for refrigeration, although many environmental chambers were already operating with liquid nitrogen. Aerosols, such as freezer sprays for electrical testing, were also found to be based on CFCs. This general survey confirmed the consumption estimates mentioned earlier, and the company moved to a phased policy to replace all CFCs.

Short-term actions

The company's first action was to raise awareness of the policy to staff at all levels. The use of CFC products for cold hand cleaning or defluxing was immediately banned as isopropyl alcohol was equally effective and could be introduced rapidly. Vapour degreasing plant was checked for leaks, location (i.e. draught free), emptying and filling practices (i.e. pumps preferred), and drag-out minimization (i.e. through correct orientation of work pieces). Recovery of ozone depleting substances was required and for remaining refrigeration applications a special recovery system was installed.

Lower CFC solvents, then recently launched on the market, were introduced, despite some problems with regard to materials compatibility with inks, paints, varnishes and plastics. Change to the new types could only be introduced following a full evaluation of possible side-effects, and ways of dealing with them established. Mistakes could be costly.

The introduction of these relatively simple measures reduced annual CFC consumption to 15 500 litres in 1990 and 14 800 litres by 1991.

Long-term strategy

An initial study indicated the necessary capital investment required to achieve the phase-out target, and this was accepted by senior management. Trials were also essential to identify potential problems in good time for solutions to be found.

Fluxes could not readily be changed and alternatives were required for removing them. Ultrasonic agitation was tried but was not sufficiently effective or reliable. Compatibility tests with other solvents were carried out and water based cleaning with water soluble fluxes had to be rejected due to high running costs, need for effluent treatment plant and long drying times. More attractive was isopropyl alcohol (IPA) which finally proved to be the most promising replacement solvent, although some proprietary solvents based on glycol ethers and esters also showed promise, particularly as a pre-clean before use of IPA. A change to IPA was found to be possible with small changes in production techniques and the cost implications were acceptable, so a full two-year evaluation commenced in 1991.

The way forward

The outcome of the evaluation was to combine the use of nitrogen inert soldering (soldering in a very low partial pressure of oxygen) with subsequent IPA cleaning. Six IPA cleaners were purchased at a cost of about £200K.

This policy led to the following additional advantages:

- Decreased solvent costs: IPA costs 20 per cent of some CFCs
- Less demanding cleaning requirements and times
- Dry printed circuit boards immediately ready for testing
- Low solder dross

- Reduction in downtimes
- No need for effluent treatment plant
- Reduced cost of cleaning per board
- Relatively low energy demands
- No additional safety controls required

As well as introducing IPA cleaning of printed circuit boards, current metal degreasing and de-watering operations based on CFCs and trichloroethane (another ODS) are being replaced with trichloroethylene which is a non-ODS substance.

These actions are now implemented, and with the use of liquid nitrogen for refrigeration enable virtually all use of ODS to be eliminated. Timetables were met well ahead of requirements from UK and EEC legislation, and products meet the all expected contractual requirements and proposed US labelling laws.

The policy of changing from CFCs to less harmful substances is an example of the first stage in the hierarchy of 'waste minimization'. However, the example of CFCs provides a cautionary note that it would be unwise for this book to recommend replacement refrigerants or similar substances, lest they present environmental risks as yet unknown.

---

4   The Environmental Problem of Ozone Enrichment

It is perhaps paradoxical that at the same time as a depletion in stratospheric ozone has occurred, there has been an increase in ozone at ground level (tropospheric ozone). This example illustrating the widespread reaction to concerns over atmospheric ozone problems is also able to link with economic benefits from environmental protection measures. The automotive industry, in common with many other sectors, is concerned about the pretreatment and coating of metal surfaces and the resulting emissions of volatile organic compounds. The concerns over these releases relate to their involvement in the complex chemical reactions leading to ozone enrichment at ground level. Increasing legislative pressures are driving the application of the hierarchy of waste management to prevent or minimize the release of volatile organic compounds.

In the case of volatile organics, the first step in an organization is to improve the raw material balance. This means determining exactly how much raw material is input to the process and how much material output occurs. Improving this balance in an automotive company involved questioning how the function was achieved, in a similar manner to that described in Chapter 6. The pollution prevention plan followed the hierarchy:

● Increasing the solids content of paints or using alternative paint formulations based on aqueous solvents. It is also possible to improve the efficiency of paint application, which controlled experiments showed had been only 38 per cent efficient in delivering paint to the product.
● Investigate ways of recycling solvents
● Destruction of unavoidable waste volatile organics.

This so-called solvent management plan involves identifying and quantifying all solvents used, and reducing their use and emissions as much as is technically feasible within economic criteria. Future actions to reduce solvent use are planned.

The company demonstrated that by planning ahead of legislation, they are ready to compete in an environmentally aware market. Companies are always concerned about what their competitors are being asked to do both in the home and overseas markets. This example shows that wherever one operates, the changes need not be dramatic, nor expensive, but can yield great benefits. The long-term proposals put forward by this company in seeking authorizations to operate under environmental legislation were costed at £65 000, but would yield savings of £450 000 overall.

5 Managing Infectious Waste

In 1992 there was a much publicized scandal in France after claims that German hospital waste was being dumped at unlicensed sites in France under the guise of domestic waste. Doubts exist that illegal traffic actually took place, and some evidence claims that the waste was actually plastic waste exported from Germany, where the plastic treatment facilities have been overwhelmed by the legislation on packaging waste to which we have referred several times. There is no doubt, however, that hospital waste presents a serious problem and may be regarded as a generic name commonly used for infectious wastes that are generated from a variety of sources, not exclusively hospitals, and many of which seem, at first sight, to be relatively innocuous (Table 8.1). A pharmacy in a typical hospital illustrates an activity subject to multiple constraints (Figure 8.1) and generating a variety of wastes for disposal.

Safe methods of disposal are needed for unwanted medicines and their containers. These medicines may be returned from wards and deemed unsuitable for recycling and require disposal, along with out of date stock and medicines brought in by patients for destruction. The preferred method for destruction

Table 8.1 Sources of infectious waste

Hospitals	General medical practitioners
Dental surgeries	Residential homes with medical services
Local authorities	Schools
Colleges and universities	Police stations
Animal boarding kennels	Cosmetic piercers (jewellers, hairdressers)
Tattooists	Acupuncturists
Beauticians	Pharmacy retail premises
Opticians	Occupational health clinics in industry, etc
Ambulance and fire services	Farming and abbatoirs
Chiropodists	Other activities, e.g. shipping

of cytotoxic drugs is incineration at 1000 °C, while a similar route is preferred for other materials that may reach the pharmacy, such as body fluid samples, blood products, used syringes and needles, any of which may present hepatitis or HIV risks. Infectious waste therefore provides a good example of waste requiring particular care in its handling throughout the route from generation to disposal.

The apparently small amounts of infectious waste likely to be generated in many of the smaller organizations may lead them to believe that it is acceptable to 'lose' it within domestic type waste. However, there are likely to be legal obligations of a duty of care for such waste, and producers need to be aware of

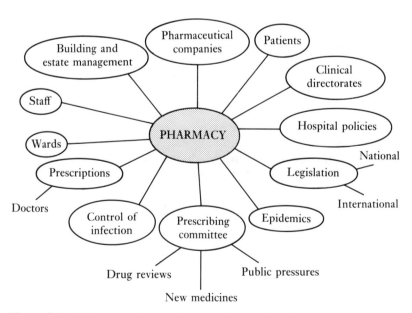

Figure 8.1 External constraints acting on a pharmacy in a hospital

them. This is notably so in the UK, where a duty of care is a legal requirement in the disposal of all commercial or industrial waste, and any waste producer must be satisfied that the waste is handled, transported and disposed of by contractors in a manner that prevents risk of harm.

One concern among waste producers may be that infectious waste incurs a premium charge for disposal, but this need not be significant if good waste management practice, leading to a substantial reduction in quantity and volume requiring specialist treatment, is adopted throughout. Following our hierarchy (Figure 8.2), we should first review whether the waste is waste. Can it be reused, perhaps after washing and resterilization? If not, perhaps the quantities can be reduced, with a consequent saving in both raw material and

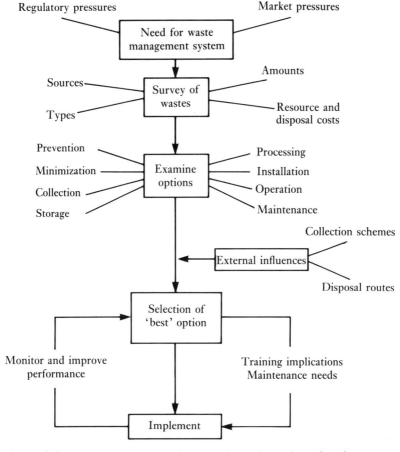

Figure 8.2 Applying an integrated waste reduction hierarchy to clinical wastes

disposal costs. Pharmaceutical waste again serves as an example with many opportunities for reducing the quantities of such waste. For example, patients in hospital traditionally use medicines supplied by the hospital while they are in-patients, with their own medicines being destroyed by incineration. As a consequence, the same medicines often had to be dispensed when the patient was discharged from hospital. By returning the patients' original medicines to them the purchase, disposal and manufacturing costs are reduced and the disposal problem reduced also. In some cases, patients may use their own medicines while in hospital, and this again reduces the amounts of waste. Ensuring that overprescribing does not occur is another important opportunity, while improved stock control through computer technology, and taking factors into account other than merely the cost of purchasing provide further routes to reducing waste for disposal. It should be clear from Figure 8.1, however, that the challenge is one of influencing all sources of such waste.

Finally, and perhaps most important, is there effective segregation of infectious waste from general waste? It has been common for some hospitals to consign wastes such as old newspapers and periodicals, as well as dead flowers, to the infectious waste route, thereby increasing their disposal quantities up to tenfold. A major drive to improve segregation in Germany has been so successful that German hospitals appear to produce less than half the infectious waste traditionally produced by establishments of similar size in the UK. However, advocating segregation presumes that it is done effectively to avoid creating new problems.

The next step in effective management is to review the local collection arrangements. Traditionally this has been in a simple plastic sack, distinguished by colour or a label. Such sacks have low physical strength, and items such as needles and broken glass, which should in any case be packed separately, can easily puncture the plastic and put handlers at risk. Moreover, the temptation to drug addicts to raid such sacks cannot be ignored.

Purpose designed, one trip containers which can be sealed at the point of dispatch are to be recommended. These containers could be strong cardboard boxes, sealed with tape which cannot be removed without leaving visible damage to the packaging, but more effective is a plastic bin with a lid which when pressed home cannot be removed. There are many advantages of these two types of packaging. They are leak and puncture-proof, have good impact resistance and can be moved safely and without causing offence over long distances for safe disposal. Once sealed, the containers also prevent contact of the contents by non-medical staff, and are safe from interference by animals.

In most countries, notification of movements of infectious waste is required, and as with any waste, it is important that descriptions are comprehensive and accurate. Copies should be given to carriers and to the disposal company, as well as to the regulators, while the disposal company should have a procedure for feedback to the producer that disposal has indeed taken place in a safe manner at an appropriate site.

Transport of infectious waste to the disposal site may take some time if the sophisticated disposal facilities required by such waste are remote from the source. Infectious wastes are biologically active and are inherently capable of becoming putrescent, and rapid delivery or temperature controlled transport appropriate for the carriage of perishable goods are essential if problems are to be avoided.

The final disposal tends to be by landfill or incineration, although novel techniques like UV sterilization or microwave heating are gaining acceptance. There is a general appreciation that landfill alone does not afford a safe and effective option for infectious waste. Whatever containers are used there is a risk of damage in emplacement and subsequent compaction, with a consequent risk of immediate harm to site personnel or long-term harm to the general public. Over time, some containers may degrade, allowing organisms to breed or offensive items such as body parts to become exposed, especially when redevelopment of the site takes place after, perhaps, a relatively short time. Options whereby infectious waste is sterilized and macerated before landfill offer advantages, but are costly and involve operations which can allow contamination of plant or personnel.

The other disposal route, incineration, has a bad reputation as a result of some hospitals and similar establishments operating small installations which have been ill-maintained and operated by relatively unskilled staff. Lack of training contributes to poor site housekeeping, failure to wear appropriate protective clothing, overloading of furnaces, and neglect of smoke or low temperature alarms. Concern to economize on fuel leads to inadequate start-up temperatures, with consequent black smoke. Routine operation at too low a temperature in the main furnace or extinguishing burners in secondary combustion chambers also results in incomplete combusion, black smoke and the risk of not destroying all the infectious components. Including large amounts of plastic waste, especially PVC, in the furnace charge can also lower the incineration temperature and fail to deal with all the microrganisms present. Similarly a high moisture content or shielding by layers of wet waste can prevent burn out, as can intermittent use of the incinerator, which results in temperature gradients. These problems tend to be greatest for small incinerators, which consequently are unable to meet prescribed emission limits, and cause significant environmental pollution and public concern. What is the solution?

The effective way of dealing with wastes of this type is to use a relatively large (1 tonne per hour or greater) incinerator dedicated to infectious waste and other hazardous wastes with similar combustion characteristics, operated over relatively long runs by competent, well-trained staff. A typical modern incinerator sytem meeting current regulatory requirements is illustrated

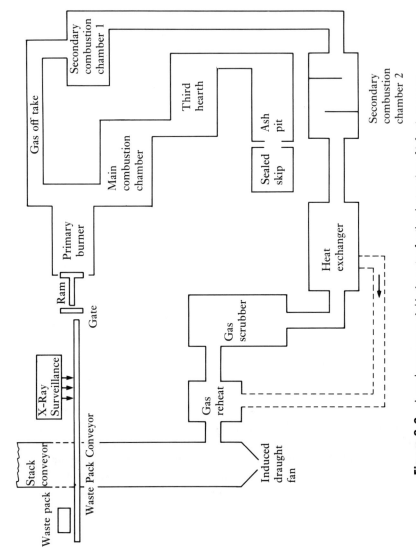

Figure 8.3 A modern commercial incinerator for the destruction of infectious waste

diagrammatically in Figure 8.3 and we can use this example to illustrate how modern pollution prevention techniques can be applied at all stages; from collection and handling, through efficient combustion to minimize the generation of pollutants, and finally by the application of control with end-of-pipe techniques.

On arrival in refrigerated vehicles, waste is weighed and consignment notes checked to ensure that the waste is the same as when it left the producer's site. Wastes are not accepted if there is any discrepancy. Consignments in sealed, one-trip containers are unloaded to conveyors feeding the incinerator or held temporarily in refrigerated containers. The delivery vehicles are then washed externally and jet cleaned before returning for further waste.

The feed conveyors are interlocked against overload, have provision for non-intrusive inspection, and reweighing of the containers in transit determines the feed rate to the furnace and the cumulative total load. Interlocks on the feed system prevent loading of any waste while the combustion chamber is below 1000 °C. Primary combustion takes place in a three hearth, gas-fired incineration unit, although a modern rotary hearth would be equally effective. Containers move from the upper to lower hearths by a series of rams, which break up the solids and ensure that all surfaces are exposed for combustion. Eight hours is the minimum residence time of solids in these combustion zones, and combustion gases then pass to the two-stage secondary combustion chamber. There pyrolysed gases, assisted by a gas burner, maintain a temperature of 1000 °C , with a forced draught fan providing about 6 per cent excess oxygen. Gases are resident in this secondary stage for at least 2 seconds, after which they pass to a heat exchanger which reduces their temperature from 1000 °C to about 250 °C. All of these steps so far have been aimed at ensuring good combustion and avoiding the generation of unnecessary air pollutants from the combustion process. Inevitably, combustion products are generated and must be treated before release to atmosphere.

Gas cleaning involves quenching, followed by a two-stage alkaline scrubbing stage in which continuous monitoring of the pH ensures that its scrubbing effectiveness is maintained. Particulate matter is retained in a settling tank and the final exhaust gases discharge from a 30 m stack. Reheating before discharge avoids the formation of a steam plume, and the heat for this is taken from the heat exchanger on the secondary combustion chamber. The remaining surplus heat is available for power generation.

Ash is continuously cleared from the hearths by rams and is delivered to skips which are sealed to prevent escape of fly-ash. The ash, particulate matter, supernatant liquids and inert solids from the whole process are taken to appropriate landfill sites for disposal under regulatory control. Landfill now represents the best practicable environmental option since the waste has been sterilized and its bulk reduced considerably.

6   Oxygen for Combustion and Pollution Prevention

In this study we see the impact of environmental constraints on an organization to bring about environmental benefits without the conventional financial benefits. It is well known that oxygen in air supports combustion, but that almost 80 per cent by volume of air is made up of nitrogen. By burning fuel in oxygen rather than air, and so keeping nitrogen out of a furnace, it is possible to cut emissions of nitrogen oxides, which are increasingly the target of regulatory standards. Additional benefits are that combustion plant can be smaller, thereby consuming less raw materials and natural resources, as well as being less expensive, while flue gas volumes are also reduced. These benefits have not been lost sight of by glass manufacturers, who use pure oxygen for their high temperature glass melting furnaces. While the approach is not universally applicable as yet, another application has been developed for waste recovery at a Teesside works of ICI in the UK, through a collaborative venture with the French company L'Air Liquide.

Methyl methacrylate (MMA) and related monomers are key raw materials used in the production of acrylic polymers such as Perspex® as well as in resins and paints. ICI's process, used for over 90 per cent of world MMA production, generates around 3 tonnes of by-product acid (BPA), containing sulphuric acid, ammonium sulphate and water, for every tonne of MMA produced.[3]

Historically, around 60 per cent of the 300 000 te/y of BPA from the monomer production process was converted to low grade fertilizer, for which only a limited market existed. The remainder of the BPA was disposed of at sea, with a small proportion to the River Tees, under Government licence and according to strict controls. Although research over many years indicated no environmental impact from disposal at sea, the need for a more socially acceptable disposal route for BPA was recognized. A planned doubling of monomer production capacity, to meet expected product demand, served only to emphasize this need.

The approach chosen by ICI to deal with the BPA disposal was based on an already established technique of high temperature oxidation of the acid, in a reactor (furnace) heated directly by combustion of either oil or gas in air. However, ICI working with l'Air Liquide, further developed the process by using pure oxygen for combustion, thereby generating a gas stream much richer in sulphur dioxide, which is then converted to sulphuric acid in a conventional process (Figure 8.4). The acid so produced is recycled into monomer production, eliminating disposal and vastly reducing the amount of fresh sulphuric acid (traditionally produced from sulphur burning) required for monomer production.

Figure 8.4 The l'Air Liquide/ICI waste treatment process (Courtesy of ICI plc)

The acid regeneration plant (Figure 8.5), accounted for almost 60 per cent of the cost of the new production facilities. The process does produce some raw material savings, although it would not meet the normal industry payback levels required for investment. However, it is an innovative approach to environmental improvement, in a traditional and conservative industry. The overall energy efficiency of the process gives approximately 30 per cent reduction in carbon dioxide emissions even after allowing for the energy for ogygen production. This justified recognition and financial support from the EU Thermie programme, which supports the demonstration of novel energy saving technologies.

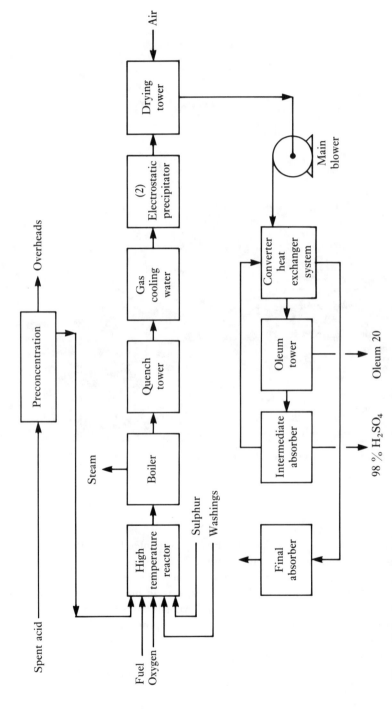

Figure 8.5 Flow diagram of the acid regeneration plant (Courtesy ICI plc)

152

7   Some Lessons from Management Conflicts

In a previous chapter we highlighted the role of management and have repeatedly emphasized that this is an important feature of an environmental management system. However, guidelines which focus on operational aspects are of little benefit to senior managers, who do not function by following manuals. They have to deal with ambiguities, uncertainties and conflicts. Organizations will respond to environmental pressures in different ways, and in the following examples we summarize some reactions from individuals in a variety of companies.

Company A: responding to the challenges of integrating environmental management

This company is involved in large scale power engineering. As in previous organizations we have described there is a company environmental policy, with ultimate responsibility vested in main board members, while site managers have day-to-day responsibility for environmental issues. An environmental manual was created in 1991 followed by extensive training courses to cascade awareness of both the policy and procedures throughout the company. Key elements of the approach include:

- A life cycle approach for each product function and service.
- Health and safety and quality assurance to be interlinked with environmental management, with care to ensure that improvements in one area do not prejudice another.
- Identification of personnel by job title to have responsibility for compliance with policy.
- Training of all staff.
- Self-audits supported by independent audits carried out by company specialists responsible for company policy.

The overall structure is one of line responsibility for control and compliance, but supported by independent company specialists. This appears to have been generally successful, although there are some doubts about the abilities of some managers to relate to what are often technical issues. This places a burden on the small number of specialists to recognize these areas of weakness and to make an appropriate response.

The company operates in a business sector in which quality management is essential, and has based its environmental management system on one of quality. The weakness of this approach, however, is that while regulatory authorities and customers in the sector demand quality management systems, the demand for environmental management systems has still to evolve to the same degree. Conflicting pressures may therefore take their toll on the continual improvement in environmental performance. This has been the case during the recession of recent years, so that again we have a company complying with rather than leading the field on environmental requirements. Nevertheless, the environmental pressures impacting on this industry will never allow it to ignore environmental issues such as the noise and emission levels caused by its product. These demands from regulators and customers call for technological developments in product design. These in turn require more exotic and high strength materials manufactured to high standards. These add to the environmental problems of manufacture. The dilemma is that market and regulatory pressures are driving towards more environmentally friendly products, but the technologies required to produce them are more energy intensive and demand scarce resources compared with the previous generation of product.

Company B: torn between targets

All organizations are subject to financial pressures, and have always considered financial implications of their actions. Unfortunately, the fact that environmental costs and benefits have rarely been quantified has been a contributory factor to the traditional failure to integrate environmental considerations into business decision-making. Managers, especially in small and medium sized enterprises, often regard it as unreasonable to spend more and more of their time on non-productive activity. They fail to recognize that good environmental management can translate into competitive advantage, and this lack of vision may not be improved by deficiencies in the environmental management system under which they operate.

Company B, in common with many during recessionary periods, operated a loss making plant among its many international activities. The result of this was that employees at the plant were forced into reactive management and found themselves searching for quick solutions to achieve production targets, with no encouragement on environmental issues such as audit matters. The environmental specialist in this situation has a potentially unenviable position, with two reporting structures. Local issues are dealt with through site management structure, while incidents, etc., are reported through to the parent company in the USA (Figure 8.6).

Adverse reports through the environmental co-ordinator route to the main board reflect badly on local management, with the result that there is an inevitable temptation to censor reports. Local site goals on environmental performance do not exist beyond those imposed from the European headquarters. The system has two inherent defects. Headquarters staff are not aware of local needs and constraints, and local staff are left with an impression that they are not trusted and empowered with responsibility. Structures and communication systems clearly could be improved, and corporate developments indicate that

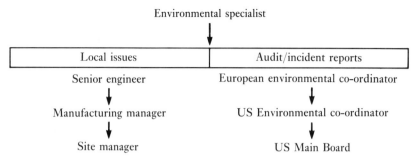

Figure 8.6   The conflict of dual reporting routes

this may be taking place. Similarly it appears that environmental training for all employees may be improved, and hopefully will increase the total of eight hour training provided for the environmental specialist over a three year period.

This example illustrates the view held by many that in a recessionary climate an environmental management programme is a luxury. Legislative pressures such as the European eco-management and audit scheme may become mandatory in the future and this scenario would change the business environment. However as we have seen many times in this book, the pressures to surpass regulatory compliance are often the result of employee and public concerns, wider company policies and increasing recognition of the commercial benefits that can ensue.

Company C: winning staff commitment

This company wishes to be regarded as one with a very responsible attitude to environmental issues, and beyond compliance with its legal obligations, it seeks to project a good image to the local community. The nature, scale and continuous operation of its activities place it firmly in the category of a potentially major polluter, but it seeks to reduce impacts. Against this, the company operates in an intensely competitive market in which margins are kept low.

A company environmental statement was issued in 1991 and begins by recognizing 'that it is important to consider environmental issues as part of its overall business strategy'. It goes on to describe the responsibilities of senior management and of committees, and requires risk assessments of each business, annual environmental audits and emergency plans.

While this company has expended a great deal of effort in developing its policy and management system, there are always opportunities to improve. In particular, there are no quantifiable objectives set, and the spirit of the policy is understood by most personnel to be one of seeking to avoid prosecution. This focus on threats rather than opportunities could be addressed by improving communication and training throughout the company. The importance of this is reinforced by the observation that while commitment is called for from the top of the company, responsibility is vested in a small number of middle managers, while operational staff actually make things happen. The company image and reputation is in their hands when they have to deal with an incident, and so full consultation, communication and training are imperatives. At the middle management level there is also a need for more training because in some plants the responsible person lacks the required technical background.

References

1   'Cleaner Production Worldwide', UNEP IE/PAC, Tour Mirabeau, Paris, 1993.
2   British Leather Confederation, *Clean Technology in the Leather Industry* (the Newsletter of the Tanning Network dedicated to improving information on clean processing methods), no. 2, January 1993, British Leather Confederation, Northampton, UK.
3   Technical information from M. Sellars of ICI Acrylics is gratefully acknowledged for this case study.

Appendix 1

Environmental Audit Checklists

The checklists that follow provide a means of reviewing environmental performances. Key elements of an environmental management system are highlighted in the reviews, and a detailed examination of waste products is prompted.

Organization Description

- Organization.
- Department.
- Product/services.
- Outline of the organization's structure, showing relationships between departments and external links.
- Flow diagrams to show inputs and outputs to and from the main processes and activities. Include service functions, e.g. cleaning and maintenance.

Known Environmental Problems

	Complaints—from whom and source	Solution applied and effectiveness		
		Prevention	Off-site reuse	Other option
General appearance/land contamination				
Solid waste: domestic industrial				
Hazardous waste				
Air pollution: smoke odours dust and grit others				
Water pollution: oils odours fish kills other				
Noise				

Environmental Management System

	Status			Location of documents and responsible person
	In existence	Proposed	Not planned	
Written policy statement				
System integrated into organization				
Register of legislation				
Register of environmental effects				
Objectives set with targets				
Programme in place				
Reference manual prepared				
Performance measurements and records				
Internal control				
Reporting: internal external				
Environmental training				
Verification				

Relevant Environmental Legislation

Legislation	Authorization/consent/licence, etc.	Date issued	Date of renewal	Changes since issue	Location of documents/responsible person

Processes and Activities

	Full information?	Up-to-date information?	Date of revisions	Location of documents/responsible person
Process description				
Process flow diagram				
Diagram of instrumentation				
Flow measurements				
Analytical data				
Energy balance				
Materials balance				
Waste analyses				
Records of releases				
Product data				
Product safety data				
Raw material composition data				
Raw material safety data				
Energy audit report				
Environmental audit report				
Operator training records				

Product/Service Design Data

	Notes	Responsible person
What is the function of the product/service?		
Have changes been made?		
Can the same function be done in a manner likely to cause less harm to the environment?		
What materials are used?		
What is the environmental impact of these materials?		
What is the environmental impact of alternative materials?		
Can a common presentation of the environmental impact allow comparison of the materials?		
Can the product be repaired?		
How many components are involved?		
How long is required for disassembly?		
What is the lifespan of the product?		
Can the components that determine the lifespan be replaced easily?		
Can the product, components or raw materials be reused?		
How can the potential for reuse be increased?		
What problems may result from reuse?		
How can these problems be eliminated or reduced?		
Can components be labelled to facilitate reuse or recycling?		
How may life cycle analysis be used to aid management decisions?		

Analysis of the Supply Chain

	Analysis of input material for each process/activity (excluding supplementary materials in next column)	Analysis of input materials not appearing in product (e.g. cleaning materials, lubricants, packaging, etc.) Indicate on flow diagram	Analysis of material in product
Material			
Function			
Active component			
Additional component			
Component(s) with potential to cause harm to the environment			
Nature of potential harm			
Annual consumption of material			
Annual use of harmful component			
Mode of delivery (drum, road tanker, etc.)			
Internal mode of transport (e.g. fork-lift truck)			
Packaging (drum, plastic, paper, etc.)			
Storage (stack, in open, silo, etc.)			
Stock management (rotation)			
Control of spills			
Useful life of material			
Where does material go after useful life?			
Where does packaging go?			
Can material and packaging go back to supplier or alternative supplier?			
Which alternative suppliers/ organizations offer disposal facilities?			
Is an audit of disposal routes offered by suppliers?			
What alternative materials are possible?			
Is different product specification acceptable to customers? Will customers accept different packaging?			

Analysis of Each Waste Stream

Process/activity
Chemical and physical characteristics of the waste
Hazardous components and concentrations
Relevant regulations and standards
Continuous or instantaneous release
Estimated rate of generation
What is the source of the waste stream?
How is the waste stream generated?
Is the waste stream segregated?
What treatment is applied to the waste stream?
What reuse/material reclamation/energy reclamation is applied?
What are the disposal costs?
What financial benefits could accrue from reuse/reclamation?
What options exist for waste prevention?
When were the options investigated?
How are new options identified?
Carry out financial appraisal of options

Appendix 2

Duty of Care: The Basic Requirements

Who is Affected?

Those who produce, import, store, treat, process, transport, recycle or dispose of any household, commercial or industrial waste, such as waste from a house, shop, office, factory, building site or any other business premises. House-holders are *not* under a Duty of Care for waste produced in their own homes by anyone living there.

What You Must Do If You Have Waste

The duty of care[1] requires you to take all reasonable steps to look after any waste you have and prevent its illegal disposal by others. Breaking the law can result in a fine for an unlimited amount.

When you have waste your first duty is to stop it escaping. Store it safely and securely.

If you hand waste on to someone else you must secure it, i.e. place it in a suitable container. Loose material placed in a skip should be covered.

You must also check that the person taking the waste away is legally entitled to do so. The following are so authorized:

- Council waste collectors. For most shops and small offices the council collect waste. In this case no more checking is necessary.
- Registered waste carriers. Most carriers of waste (other than charities and some voluntary organizations) in the UK have to be registered. Make sure the carrier has a certificate of registration. Check with the council who issued it that the registration is genuine: it will be on their register.
- Holders of waste disposal or waste management licences. Some licences are only valid for certain kinds of waste, or certain activities. Check that the licence covers your waste. There are some exemptions from having a licence, but these are very specific and you will need to check with the waste disposal authority that the exemption applies to any particular case.

Hand over a written description of the waste, with as much detail as someone else might need to handle the waste safely. In addition, fill in (and both parties must sign) a transfer note before the carrier removes the waste. The transfer note must include:

- What the waste is and the quantity.
- The type of container it is in.
- The time and date the waste was transferred.
- Where the transfer took place.
- The names and addresses of both parties.
- Details of which category of authorized person each one is.
- If either or both parties, as a waste carrier, has a registration certificate, the certificate number and the name of the council that issues it.
- Similarly, if either or both parties has a waste licence, the licence number and the name of the council that issued it.
- Reasons for any exemption from the requirement to register or have a licence.

Both parties must keep copies of the description and the transfer note for two years. They may have to prove in court where the waste came from and what they did with it.

What You Must Do If You Receive Waste from Someone Else

- First, you must be legally authorized to accept the waste, as described above.
- Second, you must get the written description from the other person, and both parties must sign a completed transfer note.

If Things Go Wrong

You must take action if you suspect that someone else is dealing with waste illegally, before or after it reaches you. Tell your local council if you are suspicious.

Reference

1   For more detailed guidance the reader is advised to consult *The Duty of Care, a Code of Practice*, HMSO, London, 1992, ISBN 011 75 25 57X.

Appendix 3

Sources of Information

Selected Professional Bodies Able to Provide Environmental Information

Telephone numbers given are those applicable from 16 April 1995.

British Effluent and Water Association
    5 Castle Street
    High Wycombe
    Bucks HP13 6RZ   01494 444 544

British Geological Survey
    Keyworth
    Nottingham NG12 5GG   01159 77 6111

British Oil Spill Control Association
    32–38 Lemam Street
    London E1 8EW   0171 928 9199

British Reclamation Industries Federation
    16 High Street
    Brampton, Huntingdon
    Cambridgeshire PE18 8TU   01480 455 249

Centre for Environmental Technology
    Imperial College of Science, Technology & Medicine
    48 Prince's Gardens
    London Sw7 1LU   0171 589 5111

Centre for International Environmental Law
    King's College
    Manresa Road
    London SW3   0171 352 8123

Centre for Remote Sensing
    Imperial College of Science, Technology & Medicine
    Prince Consort Road
    London SW7 2BZ   0171 589 5111

Confederation of British Industry
    Centre Point
    103 New Oxford Street
    London WC1A 1DU   0171 379 7400

Department of the Environment
    2 Marsham Street
    London SW1P 3EB   0171 276 3000

Department of Trade & Industry
    123 Victoria Street
    London SW1E 6RB   0171 215 5000

Environmental Information Centre
    Institute of Terrestrial Ecology
    Monks Wood Experimental Station
    Huntingdon,
    Cambridgeshire PE17 2LS   0148 73381

Freshwater Biological Association
    The Ferry house
    Far Sawrey
    Ambleside, Cumbria LA22 0LP   019662 2468

Friends of the Earth
    26–28 Underwood Street
    London N1 7JQ   0181 490 1555

Geological Society
    Burlington House
    Piccadilly
    London W1V 0JU   0171 434 9944

Greenpeace
    30–31 Islington Green
    London N1 8XE   0181 354 5100

Health & Safety Commission/ Health & Safety Executive
    Baynards House
    1 Chepstow Place
    Westbourne Grove
    London W2 4TF   0171 243 6000

Her Majesty's Inspectorate of Pollution
    Romney House
    43 Marsham Street
    London SW1P 3PY   0171 276 3000
    (To be incorporated in Environmental Agency)

Hydrological Society
    The Institution of Civil Engineers
    Great George Street
    London SW1P 3AA   0171 630 0726

Institute of Hydrology
    Maclean Building
    Crowmash Gifford
    Wallingford, Oxon OX10 8BB   01491 838 800

Institute of Packaging
    Sysonby Lodge
    Nottingham Road
    Melton Mowbray
    Leicestershire LE13 0NU   01664 500 055

Institute of Waste Management
    3 Albion Place
    Northampton NN1 1UD   01604 20426

Institute of Water & Environmental Management
    15 John Street
    London WC1N 2EB   0171 831 3110

Institution of Chemical Engineers
    George Davis Building
    165–171 Railway Terrace
    Rugby CV21 3HQ   01788 578214

Institution of Environmental Health Officers
    Chadwick House
    Rushworth Street
    London SE1 0RB   0171 928 6006

Institution of Environmental Sciences
    14 Princes Gate
    Hyde Park
    London SW7 1PU   01252 515 511

International Atomic Energy Agency
   PO Box 100
   Wagramerstrasse 5
   1400 Vienna, Austria   1-0222-2360

International Maritime Organization
   4 Albert Embankment
   London SE1 7SR   0171 735 7611

International Union of Air Pollution Prevention Associations
   136 North Street
   Brighton, BN1 1RG   01273 26313

Meteorological Office
   Sutton Building
   London Road
   Bracknell, Berks RG12 2SZ   01344 854 818

National Association of Waste Disposal Contractors
   26 Wheatsheaf House
   4 Carmelite Street
   London EC4Y 0BN   0171 353 1961

National Radiological Protection Board
   Chilton, Didcot
   Oxon OX11 0RQ   01235 831 600

National Remote Sensing Centre
   Space Department
   Royal Aerospace Establishment
   Farnborough
   Hampshire GU14 6TD   01252 541 464

National Rivers Authority
   Rivers House
   Waterside Drive
   Aztec West
   Almondsbury
   Bristol BS12 4UD   01454 624400
   (To be incorporated in Environmental Agency)

National Society for Clean Air & Environmental Protection
   136 North Street
   Brighton BN1 1RG   01273 26313

Natural Environment Research Council
　　Polaris House
　　North Star Avenue
　　Swindon, Wiltshire SN2 1EU　　01793 411623

Noise Abatement Society
　　PO Box 8
　　Bromley, Kent BR2 0UH　　0181 460 3146

Open University Energy & Environmental Group
　　Walton Hall
　　Milton Keynes
　　Buckinghamshire MK7 6AA　　01908 653 335

Royal Commission on Environmental Pollution
　　Church House
　　Great Smith Street
　　London SW1 3BL　　0171 276 2080

Royal Institute of Public Health & Hygiene
　　28 Portland Place
　　London W1N 4DE　　0171 580 2731

Royal Society
　　6 Carlton House Terrace
　　London SW1Y 5AG　　0171 839 5561

Royal Society of Chemistry
　　Burlington House,
　　Piccadilly,
　　London W1V 0BN　　0171–437–8656

Royal Society for Nature Conservation
　　The Green
　　Nettleham
　　Lincoln LN2 2NR　　01522 752326

UK Environmental Law Association
　　Masons, Solicitors
　　116/118 Chancery Lane
　　London WC2A 1AP　　0171 583 9990

United Nations Environmental Programme
　　PO Box 30552
　　Nairobi
　　Kenya　　2-333930

United Nations Environmental Programme
    Industry and Environment Activity Centre (UNEP IE/PAC)
    39–43 Quai André Citroën
    73739 Paris
    Cedex 15
    France   33(1)44 37 14 50

United States Environmental Protection Agency
    401 M St, SW
    Washington, DC 20460   202-382-2090

Water Services Association
    1 Queen Anne's Gate
    London SW1H 9BT   0171 222 8111

World Health Organization
    Avenue Appia
    1211 Geneva 27
    Switzerland   022-912-111

Directories

Several directories provide more comprehensive details of organizations concerned with environmental issues, and include the following:

A Directory of European Environmental Organizations, M. Deziron, and L. Bailey, Blackwell, Oxford, 1991.

Directory for the Environment, 2nd edition, M. J. C. Barker, Routledge & Kegan Paul, London, 1986.

Environmental Information, A Guide to Sources, N. Lees, and H. Woolston, The British Library, London, 1992.

NSCA Members Handbook, National Society for Clean Air and Environmental Protection, 136 North Street, Brighton, BN1 1RG.

World Directory of Environmental Organizations, 4th edition, T. C. Trzyna, and R. Childers (Eds). California Institute of Public Affairs in cooperation with Sierra Club and the World Conservation Union, California Institute of Public Affairs, Sacramento, California, USA, 1992.

Appendix 4

Prescribed Processes and Substances Under UK Integrated Pollution Control

These are extracted from *Environmental Protection* (*Prescribed Substances*) *Regulations 1991*, HMSO, London, 1991.

Prescribed Processes

Fuel and power industry

Combustion boilers and furnaces (> 50 MW thermal output)
Combustion (remainder)
Gasification
Carbonization
Petroleum

Waste disposal industry

Incineration
Chemical recovery
Waste derived fuel

Mineral industry

Cement
Asbestos
Fibre
Glass
Ceramic

Chemical industry

Petrochemical
Organic
Chemical pesticide
Pharmaceutical
Acid manufacturing
Halogen
Chemical fertilizer
Bulk chemical storage
Inorganic chemical

Metal industry

Iron and steel
Smelting
Non-ferrous

Other industry

Paper manufacturing
Di-isocyanate
Tar and bitumen
Uranium
Coating
Coating manufacturing
Timber
Animal and plant treatment

Exceptions

These are processes which:

- Cannot result in emissions to air, water or land of any relevant prescribed substance or will result in the release of such substance in such trivial amounts that the release cannot do harm.
- Are undertaken at a school or museum.
- Are engines to propel aircraft, vehicles ships or other vessels.
- Are carried out as a domestic activity in connection with a private dwelling.

Prescribed Substances

Releases to air

Oxides or sulfur and other sulfur compounds
Oxides of nitrogen and other nitrogen compounds
Oxides of carbon
Organic compounds and partial oxidation products
Metals, metalloids and their compounds
Asbestos (suspended particulate matter and fibres)
Glass fibres and mineral fibres
Halogens and their compounds
Phosphorus and its compounds
Particulate matter

Releases to water

Mercury and its compounds
Cadmium and its compounds
All isomers of hexachlorocyclohexane
All isomers of DDT
Pentachlorophenol and its compounds
Hexachlorobenzene
Aldrin
Endrin
Polychlorinated biphenyls
Dichlovos
1,2-Dichloroethane
All isomers of trichlorobenzene
Altrazine
Simazine
Tributyltin compounds
Triphenyltin compounds
Trifluralin
Fenithrothion
Azinphos–methyl
Malathion
Endosulfan

Releases to land

Organic solvents
Azides

Halogens and their covalent compounds

Metal carbonyls

Organometallic compounds

Oxidizing agents

Polychlorinated dibenzofuran and any cogener thereof

Polychlorinated dibenzo-*p*-dioxin and any cogener thereof

Polyhalogenated biphenyls, terphenyls and naphthalenes

Phosphorus

Pesticides, that is, any chemical substance or preparation prepared or used for destroying any pest, including those used for protecting plants or wood or other plant products from harmful organisms; regulating the growth of plants; giving protection against harmful creatures; rendering such creatures harmless; controlling oganisms with harmful or unwanted effects on water systems, buildings or other structures, or on manufactured products; or protecting animals against ectoparasites.

Alkali metals and their oxides

Alkaline earth metals and their oxides

Appendix 5

The EU Integrated Pollution Prevention and Control Directive: Pollutants and Best Available Techniques

The Most Important Polluting Substances and Preparations

Air

Sulfur dioxide and other sulfur compounds
Oxides of nitrogen and other nitrogen compounds
Carbon monoxide and dioxide
Volatile organic compounds
Heavy metals and their compounds
Dust, asbestos (suspended particulates and fibres), glass and mineral fibres
Chlorine and its compounds
Fluorine and its compounds
Arsenic and its compounds
Ammonia
Hydrogen cyanide and fluoride
Nitric acid
Substances and preparations proved to have carcinogenic properties when carried by air

Water

Organohalogen compounds and substances which may form such compounds in the aquatic environment
Organophosphorus compounds
Organotin compounds

Substances and preparations proved to have carcinogenic properties in or via the aquatic environment

Mercury and its compounds

Cadmium and its compounds

Persistent mineral oils and hydrocarbons of petroleum origin

Persistent synthetic substances which may float, remain in suspension or sink and which may interfere with any use of waters

Zinc, copper, nickel, chromium, lead, selenium, arsenic, antimony, molybdenum, titanium, tin, barium, beryllium, boron, uranium, vanadium, cobalt, thallium, tellurium, silver

Nutrients, e.g. nitrates, phosphates

Land

Wastes identified as hazardous by Article 1 of Directive 91/689/EEC.

Considerations for Selecting the Best Available Techniques

Use of low waste technologies

Increased recovery and recycling of substances generated and used in the process, where appropriate

Comparable processes, facilities or methods of operation which have recently been successfully tried out

Technological advances and changes in scientific knowledge and understanding

Nature and volume of the emissions concerned

Time limits for the installation of the techniques

Consumption of raw materials (including water) and energy used in the process and their nature

Need to prevent or minimize the overall impact of the emissions on the environment

Glossary of Abbreviations and Terms

ACBE   The Advisory Committee on Business and the Environment. A committee set up in 1991 by the UK Government to provide a dialogue between Government and business on environmental issues.

Acid deposition   Commonly known as acid rain, this includes rain, snow, fog and mist contaminated by oxides of sulphur and nitrogen, which make it acidic. Dry deposition also occurs by vegetation and surfaces removing the acidic substances from the atmosphere.

Action level   The concentration of a substance at a location, below which with present knowledge, the environmental consequences of a release can be considered negligible when assessing the BPEO.

Agenda 21   A global action plan to reconcile future developments with environmental imperatives. The Rio Declaration identifies local action as the key to success for Agenda 21.

BAT   Best Available Techniques. An abbreviation of similar meaning to BATNEEC, but the 'excessive cost' element is incorporated in the meaning of 'available'.

BATNEEC   Best Available Techniques Not Entailing Excessive Costs. An abbreviation widely used in an international context relating to environmental protection. In European Union Directives, the word 'technology' often replaces 'techniques' used in UK legislation. Techniques is intended to embrace both hardware and operational factors.

BOD   Biochemical Oxygen Demand. A measure of water pollution in terms of the oxygen required for the biological breakdown of pollutants in water.

BPEO   Best Practicable Environmental Option. The outcome of a systematic consultative and decision-making procedure which emphasizes the protection of the environment across land, air and water. The BPEO procedure establishes, for a given set of objectives, the option that provides the most benefit, or least damage, to the environment as a whole, at acceptable cost, in the long term as well as the short term.

BPEO Index   The Ranking of a series of Environmental Options and the weightings afforded to them.

Bruntland Report   Report of the 1987 World Commission on Environment and Development.

CERES See Valdez Principles.

CFC Abbreviation for chlorofluorocarbons (q.v.)

Chlorofluorocarbons A group of chemicals which have found wide use as solvents, spray-can propellants, refrigerants and foam expanders. The use of these substances is being phased out by international convention.

COD Chemical Oxygen Demand. A measure of water pollution in terms of the chemical oxidation of pollutants.

Critical load A quantitative estimate of exposure to pollutants below which no significant harmful effects are believed to result.

Discharge consent A licence granted by a regulatory body to permit the discharge of effluent of specified quality and volume.

DNA Deoxyribonucleic acid. An essential compound found in the nucleus of all living cells.

Duty of Care A legal requirement on a waste producer to make sure that all reasonable precautions are taken to ensure that waste is transported by a registered carrier for disposal at a licensed site and is disposed of in a responsible manner.

Environmental audit A systematic, documented, periodic and objective evaluation of how well environmental organization, management and equipment are performing with the aim of helping to safeguard the environment by facilitating management control of environmental practices and assessing compliance with company policies which would include meeting regulatory requirements.

Environmental Impact Assessment A formal assessment of the total environmental effects of a project, process, product or development.

EQS Environmental Quality Standard.

EU Directive A European Union (formerly European Community, EU) legal instrument identifying an outcome binding on all member states, but leaving the method of implementation to the national governments through national legislation.

EU Regulation European Union legislation having legal force in all member states.

FGD Flue gas desulphurization: a technique for the removal of sulphur oxides from the flue gas of large combustion plant such as power stations.

HAZAN Hazard Analysis.

HAZOP Hazard and Operability Study.

Heavy metals A collective term used for metals with the potential to cause harm when they are released into the environment. Typically it includes mercury, lead and cadmium, as well as zinc, chromium and certain other metals with wide industrial use and potential toxic effects.

HMIP Her Majesty's Inspectorate of Pollution. HMIP was set up in 1987 to regulate particular industrial processes ('prescribed processes') that utilize or can release high risk pollutants ('prescribed substances') with the potential to cause significant harm to the environment. HMIP enforce Integrated Pollution Control (IPC) in England and Wales. Counterpart agencies operate in Scotland (HMIPI) and Northern Ireland.

HSE Health and Safety Executive. The UK regulatory body for health and safety in the workplace. This abbreviation is also sometimes used for health, safety and environmental.

ICC Business Charter for Sustainable Development Sixteen principles for environmental management proposed by the International Chamber of Commerce and widely adopted by businesses.

IPC Integrated pollution control. A legal framework in UK legislation taking an holistic view of environmental regulation. Solutions to particular environmental problems take account of potential effects on all environmental media.

IPM Integrated pollution management. The philosophy of integrating environmental issues into the management culture of an organization.

IPPC Integrated pollution prevention and control. A regulatory concept from the European Union, in which the environment is looked at as a whole in a similar manner to the approach in IPC.

LCA Life cycle assessment. An objective process for evaluating the environmental burdens associated with a product, process or activity by identifying and quantifying the energy and material use and environmental releases. The assessment includes the entire life cycle of the product, process or activity, and encompasses extracting and processing the raw materials, manufacturing, transportation, distribution, reuse, maintenance and ultimate disposal. Other terms used are resource and environmental profile analysis (REPA), eco-profile analysis, eco-balancing and 'cradle-to-grave' analysis.

LNB Low nitrogen oxides burners.

NIMBY The acronym for the attitude 'not in my back yard'.

NRA National Rivers Authority. The regulatory organization concerned with water quality and pollution control in rivers, lakes, groundwater and coastal waters.

OECD Organization for Economic Co-operation and Development.

Ozone depleting chemicals Chemicals, such as CFCs and halons which have the potential to deplete the ozone concentration in the stratosphere. This ozone provides a protective barrier against harmful ultraviolet radiation from the sun.

PAN Peroxyacetyl nitrate. An air pollutant generated from VOCs and oxides of nitrogen under the influence of sunlight. PAN caures eye irritation and in common with other oxidants produced by a similar route causes plant injury.

Predicted Environmental Concentration The total predicted concentration of a substance expected at a given location.

Preliminary environmental site assessment (PESA)   A non-intrusive study of a site and the surrounding properties, together with a review of historical records and local knowledge with the objective of identifying potential land contamination.

RCEP   Royal Commission on Environmental Pollution.

Regulatory Assessment Level (RAL)   The long-term average concentration of a substance which for the purpose of assessing the BPEO the Regulatory Body regards as the maximum value permissible in the environmental medium concerned at that location.

Responsible Care   An initiative which began in Canada in the mid 1980s: a chemical industry programme that involves showing the public that industry is responsible about its environmental obligations, and does not put the public at risk. It aims to show that measures are put in place to effectively manage chemicals, chemical products and processes. It includes many codes of practice, including one of product stewardship, which requires accepting responsibility for products from 'the cradle to the grave'.

Sustainable development   Development that meets the needs of the present without compromising the ability of future generations to meet their own needs.

SCR   Selective catalytic reduction.

SNCR   Selective, non-catalytic reduction.

Tolerability quotient (TQ)   Derived for each substance and for each medium as the quotient of the predicted environmental concentration and the appropriate EQS or RAL. Used in the BPEO index assessment.

Valdez Principles   Principles for good environmental management produced by a coalition of US fund managers and environmentalists—the Coalition for Environmentally Responsible Economies- and named after the Exxon Valdez incident. The principles are now known as the CERES Principles.

Volatile organic compound (VOC)   An organic compound other than methane that is capable of producing secondary air pollution (e.g. ozone) by chemical reactions with oxides of nitrogen under the influence of sunlight.

Index

Clean Technology, *see* Waste
    management: clean technology
Coal-fired power station, 69
Coca-Cola, 54, 75
COD, definition, 183
Code of Environmental Ethics for
    Engineers, 127
Computer software:
  life cycle analysis, 78
  PHAROS, 47
  VISITT, 57, 66, 105
Constraints, 10, 144
Consultan, 6, 58, 59, 82, 120, 131
Contaminated land, 26, 27, 60
Control of Pollution Act, 1974, 97
Cost recovery charging, 25
Costs, 19
  and profitability, 2, 39
  capital and revenue expenditure, 20
  long term, 24, 27, 60
  non-monetary, 105
  of disposal, 56
  restoration, 26, 31
  water charges, 24, 103
Critical load, definition, 183
Croda Colours, 54
Crystal Drinks, 54
Cyclops, 93

Department of Trade and Industry, 7, 54,
    105
Design for the environment, 4
Digital Equipment Corporation, 55
Directive (EU Directive), definition, 183
Discharge consent, definition, 183
Du Pont, 115
Du Pont Howson, 54
Duty of Care, 50, 59, 61, 84, 98, 145, 163
  definition, 183

Earth Summit, 15
Eastern Counties Leather *vs* Cambridge
    Water Co, 86, 134
Emergency planning, 34
Energy efficiency, 16, 20, 32, 44, 54, 82,
    124, 139, 151
  costs as constraints, 21
Engineering Council, 127
Environment:
  communicating to the public, 52, 115
  education, 29, 30
  effects on, 3

information from the media, 112, 118
information on, 95
public attitudes, 29, 44, 111, 127, 155
public awareness, 14, 22, 28, 36, 53, 132
  local liaison group, 117, 121
staff awareness, 125, 130
technology transfer, 136
Environmental advisory board, 131
Environmental Audits, 6, 32, 39, 45,
    50, 153, 157
  definition, 45, 183
Environmental control options:
  coal-fired power station, 70
Environmental economics, 23, 99
  carbon tax, 26
  cost recovery charging, 25
  free resources, 39
  legal penalties, 25
Environmental effects, 7, 52, 67
  critical group, 68
  epidemiology, 7
  liabilities, 10
  long- *vs* short-term effects, 69
  modelling, 7, 72
  risk assessment, 8
  targets, 68
  value judgements, 14
Environmental Impact Assessment, 59,
    61, 65, 183
Environmental information:
  communication to the public, 114
    guidelines, 118
  public registers, 111
  role of the media, 112
Environmental liability, 27, 37, 60, 86,
    134
Environmental management:
  accountability, 19
  advisory boards, 131
  communications, 23, 52, 53, 111
  corporate policy, 7, 39, 52
  design for the environment, 38
  environmental audit, 6, 32, 39, 45, 50,
    153, 157
  environmental review, 51, 60
  improvement plans, 60
  individual participation, 19, 28
  involvement of production, 5
  involvement of research &
    development, 5
  involvement of sales, 5
  leadership, 19, 125, 129, 137

A Short Textbook of
ORTHOPAEDICS AND TRAUMATOLOGY

UNIVERSITY MEDICAL TEXTS

General Editor
Selwyn Taylor, D.M., M.Ch., F.R.C.S.
ROYAL POSTGRADUATE MEDICAL SCHOOL, HAMMERSMITH HOSPITAL

A Short Textbook of Medicine
Fifth Edition
J. C. Houston, M.D., F.R.C.P.
PHYSICIAN AND DEAN OF THE MEDICAL SCHOOL, GUY'S HOSPITAL
C. L. Joiner, M.D., F.R.C.P.
PHYSICIAN, GUY'S HOSPITAL
J. R. Trounce, M.D., F.R.C.P.
PROFESSOR OF THERAPEUTICS, GUY'S HOSPITAL MEDICAL SCHOOL

A Short Textbook of Surgery
Fourth Edition
Selwyn Taylor, D.M., M.Ch., F.R.C.S.
ROYAL POSTGRADUATE MEDICAL SCHOOL, HAMMERSMITH HOSPITAL
L. T. Cotton, M.Ch., F.R.C.S.
SURGEON, KING'S COLLEGE HOSPITAL

A Short Textbook of Medical Microbiology
Fourth Edition
D. C. Turk, D.M., M.R.C.P., M.C.Path
CONSULTANT MICROBIOLOGIST SHEFFIELD REGIONAL HEALTH LABORATORY
I. A. Porter, M.D., M.C.Path.
CONSULTANT BACTERIOLOGIST, CITY HOSPITAL, ABERDEEN.
HONORARY CLINICAL SENIOR LECTURER IN BACTERIOLOGY,
UNIVERSITY OF ABERDEEN.

A Short Textbook of Chemical Pathology
Third Edition
D. N. Baron, M.D., D.Sc., M.R.C.P., F.C.Path.
PROFESSOR OF CHEMICAL PATHOLOGY, ROYAL FREE HOSPITAL SCHOOL OF MEDICINE

A Short Textbook of Gynaecology and Obstetrics
G. D. Pinker, M.B., F.R.C.S., F.R.C.O.G.
CONSULTANT GYNAECOLOGICAL SURGEON AND OBSTETRICIAN, ST. MARY'S HOSPITAL
D. W. T. Roberts, M.Chir., F.R.C.S., F.R.C.O.G.
CONSULTANT OBSTETRICIAN AND GYNAECOLOGIST, ST. GEORGE'S HOSPITAL

A Short Textbook of Psychiatry
Second Edition
W. L. Linford Rees, B.Sc., M.D., F.R.C.P., D.P.M.
PROFESSOR OF PSYCHIATRY, ST. BARTHOLOMEW'S HOSPITAL MEDICAL COLLEGE, LONDON

A Short Textbook of Medical Statistics
Sir Austin Bradford Hill, C.B.E., D.Sc., Ph.D., Hon.D.Sc.(Oxon).,
Hon. M.D. (Edin.), F.F.C.M. (Hon.), F.R.C.P. (Hon.), F.R.S.
PROFESSOR EMERITUS OF MEDICAL STATISTICS, UNIVERSITY OF LONDON

A Short Textbook of Paediatrics
P. Catzel, M.B.B.Ch., F.R.C.P., D.C.H.
SENIOR PAEDIATRICIAN, TRANSVAAL MEMORIAL HOSPITAL FOR CHILDREN
JOHANNESBURG